T0209003

Praise for Career Discovery

"Heaven's kiss of inspiration is upon Jessie Lynn and this book. And it will spread to all those who seek to discover their authentic self and calling in life." - Michael Bernard Beckwith, author of *Spiritual Liberation* and *Life Visioning* and founder at Agape International Spiritual Center

"Words will fall short of describing the spirit that goes by the name of Jessie Lynn, but here goes. The sheer brilliance and radiance that this woman exudes with every fiber of her being is astonishing – she's *truly* a channel of divine wisdom and feminine power. I am THRILLED that she's put some of her magic into such a humbly disguised gift of a Career Discovery handbook. The applications and her loving support in the words on every page will transform your life – brace yourself! P.S. If you ever have the chance to work with Jessie one-on-one, please ask her to do a guided meditation for you – she removed so many blocks for me in one session that had been holding me back for nearly my whole life, and I am eternally grateful." -Regina Getz-Kikuchi, Management Scientist, Google

"Jessie has been an inspiration and light in my life. She keeps me focused on my true path and motivates me to follow my life passions. Her positive energy is infectious. I'm truly blessed to have Jessie as a friend and mentor." -Julia Stockwell, Manager at Northrop Grumman

"Jessie has a natural way of reminding others of what their souls know deep down. She has a knack for making slight adjustments that will help align you with your truth. And her gift of encouragement has personally helped me in this season of being a new mom." -Lezlie Mitchell, Writer/Actor/Model

"Jessie has played an integral role in shaping my career and quickly became the older sister I always hoped for and wanted. She is one of the most loving and generous people I have ever met - always happy and willing to give her time and energy to those who need it. Jessie truly has a passion for helping others and is always doing what she can to uplift those around her each and every day. Inspiring and empowering both men and women to follow their dreams is what she was put on this earth to do. Over the years Jessie has been there to always cheer me on and guide me through life's crazy twists and turns. I am so grateful for the wisdom she has bestowed upon me. She has helped me so much professionally, but I am most grateful for what she has done for me personally. She has always reflected back to me the person I hope to be, and as a result, I can say that she has taught me to truly love myself. Having Jessie as my mentor has been one of my greatest blessings. She is a remarkable human being. These words simply do not do justice to what an incredible mentor she is. Jessie has forever changed my life, and I know if you let her - she will do the same for you!" –Holly Bliss Hensen, Owner of Holly Bliss Art

"Jessie's influence has empowered me to go fearlessly after my dreams and stay the course to gracefully give everything in my life one hundred and twenty percent at all times. Jessie has truly been an inspiration and guiding force in making me the woman I am today and the woman I am becoming. I am blessed to have such an inspirational woman not only as a friend but a sister that sets the bar high and always shows up and leads by example. Jessie shows me time and time again that anything I want to accomplish in my life is possible just by showing up for myself every day." –Mikaela Adams, Owner at Mobile Style

"In a period of my life riddled with self-doubt regardless of years of proven ability, Jessie walked into my life and without prompting, assured me I was set for great things. At the time I thought it to be kind words of a new found friend and retreated back into my safe and protected routine. Several years later, after being faced with my own mortality at 29, it was the repeating memory of her words that fueled my fire to put everything I had worked for on the line and leave the ring of safety. Her consistent encouragement, woven into her story of persistence and inner strength, convinced me to establish my own brand. A brand that has paved the way out of a life of routine self-doubt and into one more rewarding than I can express." -Matt McGill, Owner of Ealantas

"As long as I've known Jessie, she's been a light in my life. She is sound in both physical and emotional advice and I cannot imagine my growth as an individual without her influence. She is truly a powerful female figure and an inspiration to all that meet her." –Clinton Kyles, Director, and Dancer

"Jessie is a change agent, indeed! I feel so blessed to have the pleasure and privilege to share what an absolutely transformative experience I had with Jessie! One relatively short meeting with Jessie helped guide me on my ultimate path of self-realization. I believe Jessie's energy and remarkable methods were the catalysts to ignite this eternal flame within me. Jessie helped me toward a path to inner peace and clarity. Mere words aren't sufficient to articulate her priceless contribution to my life. Thank you, Jessie, for sharing your love and light!" -H. Rene Coleman, Psychotherapist

"Jessie plays such a big part of my new life journey, my life completely changed in the best most positive way from her guidance and friendship. Her energy is so bright, it's contagious. She is a positive role model and has never steered me in the wrong direction. Her words are uplifting and I'm so grateful for her contributions in my life." -Autumn Craft, Model/Actress

"If I was allotted one word to describe Jessie's work I would use the word "transformational". I personally experienced her work and I gladly proclaim working with Jessie literally changed my life. In one session we broke down barriers that I wrestled with most of my adult life. Her natural ability to care, tap in, expose, heal, love and prompt change with grace was done in her unique one of a kind way. Jessie is a gift to our world, a force to be seen. Jessie walks in and radiates true light." -Jasmine Harris, Life Coach/Mentor

"Jessie has the ability to bring out the best in people. Her motivational words will inspire you to lead a life of confidence and pursue your life goals. True happiness and success is the goal she seeks in each individual. Jessie has personally inspired me to reach for the sky and to set goals beyond my wildest dreams." –Eba Lida, Owner of Eba Cosmetics

"Jessie has been the light in my life that has led me to lead the beautiful life I have today. She has been there for me for as long as I can remember. The only person who has encouraged, believed, and pushed me, even when I said I couldn't possibly take on another role or ask for a promotion, there was Jessie. Each time I rose higher because Jessie believed in me even when I initially wasn't able to see the ability in myself. Jessie is an amazing woman who emanates a magical aura into this world. Her gifts make a difference. I am grateful for her impact." –Caroline Venegas, Owner of Ms. Veganiese

CAREER DISCOVERY

Aligning Passions with Purpose

*A guide to activate your highest potential
and create the life you deserve*

JESSIE LYNN, MSML

BALBOA.
PRESS
A DIVISION OF HAY HOUSE

Balboa Press books may be ordered through booksellers or by contacting:

Balboa Press
A Division of Hay House
1663 Liberty Drive
Bloomington, IN 47403
www.balboapress.com
1 (877) 407-4847

Because of the dynamic nature of the Internet, any web addresses or links contained in this book may have changed since publication and may no longer be valid. The views expressed in this work are solely those of the author and do not necessarily reflect the views of the publisher, and the publisher hereby disclaims any responsibility for them.

The author of this book does not dispense medical advice or prescribe the use of any technique as a form of treatment for physical, emotional, or medical problems without the advice of a physician, either directly or indirectly. The intent of the author is only to offer information of a general nature to help you in your quest for emotional and spiritual well-being. In the event you use any of the information in this book for yourself, which is your constitutional right, the author and the publisher assume no responsibility for your actions.

Any people depicted in stock imagery provided by Getty Images are models, and such images are being used for illustrative purposes only. Certain stock imagery © Getty Images.

This book is a work of non-fiction. Unless otherwise noted, the author and the publisher make no explicit guarantees as to the accuracy of the information contained in this book and in some cases, names of people and places have been altered to protect their privacy.

Print information available on the last page.

ISBN: 978-1-9822-0742-7 (sc)
ISBN: 978-1-9822-0744-1 (hc)
ISBN: 978-1-9822-0743-4 (e)

Library of Congress Control Number: 2018907559

Balboa Press rev. date: 03/19/2019

Dedication

To my beloved daughter, Ava Lynn Montgomery: You are LIGHT, you are set apart, and you are full of infinite potential. This means that you are limitless; you can accomplish anything that you set your mind to. All you have to do is follow your inner guidance system and take inspired action. If you make a mistake, or if you find yourself in a situation that you do not want to be in, know that each day is a new opportunity to start again. You get to hit the restart button as many times as you need to. There are not rules and there are no limitations.

Create the life of your dreams, follow your bliss, and live a life worth living.

The world is your stage! Radiantly SHINE, Baby.

With infinite love,

Mommy

Contents

Part 3: Career Discovery

Preface

In 2015, I took a course at Pepperdine University while working on my masters of science degree in management and leadership. In one of the classes, I learned that a Gallup study showed that seventy percent of America's workforce is unhappy, unfulfilled, and stagnant in their careers. Hearing this alarming truth lit a fire in my heart. At that moment, it became clear that I had to do something to change the statistic and help souls wake up and see who they truly are. It became even more clear that I had to develop a body of work that would inspire people in this nation and all over the world to step into their life's calling and align their passions with purpose. Creating value for millions of people and helping people become stronger versions of themselves is my purpose. Career Discovery is the call to action to create a wave of change in this world.

I often tell the "Starfish Story"… you may have heard of it. It is the story of the little boy who walked along the beach shore. He saw that a million starfish had washed up the shore. He began to pick up starfish, one at a time, and throw them back into the water. A man noticed the little boy and approached him to learn what he was doing. Stating, "It'll be high noon soon. The sun will burn out and kill all of these starfish. You surely cannot make a difference and save them all." The little boy responded to the man by gently picking up another starfish and throwing it back into the ocean, giving it a new sense of life. The little boy with eyes full of hope and fulfillment looked up to the man and said, "I just made a difference to that one."

In the spirit of making a difference to one, I view the seventy percent of unfulfilled people working in America as beautiful starfish who are full of infinite potential. If by reading this guide, a difference is made to one person, then writing this guide will be well worth it. And if an impact is made on the masses, then my life's purpose will be fulfilled and my dream will come true.

Mentorship is my purpose. I have had the honor and privilege of serving others in this capacity for the past 10 years and it has been my greatest joy. I believe that we succeed by embracing, supporting, and leveraging our strengths and knowledge to open doors and help others succeed. This guide is an attempt to share knowledge to assist you to open the doors to the life you truly deserve.

As I mentor, my main objective with each sister/brother is the same: to assist them to realize their full potential so that they can become a stronger version of who they are. Mentorship is a gift that was entrusted to me, and I approach serving others with great care. Mentorship in my lens is simple... I view myself as everyone's soul sister, and I believe that everyone could benefit from additional support and at times, be reminded of the brilliance they truly are.

The goal of this practical guide is to support you in evolving, unfolding, and becoming purpose-driven by walking in your true brilliance. This guide will serve as a catalyst for growth, offering guidance, love, and support – all necessary to point you in the direction of practices and daily routines to incorporate in your life. Completing the exercises in this guide is how you start to embrace your journey and how you will create the life that you deserve, the life of your dreams.

It is my desire that each reader expands to the point of fulfillment. Fulfillment means that you learn to operate from your "overflow." Have you ever heard the saying, "My cup runneth over?" Well, often times, people are so committed to their daily roles, that they operate being half full. They seem to always be last on a to-do list and they operate at a fraction of their full potential because they are always tired and spread thin from all of life's demands. My desire is to put you at the top of your priorities and to guide you in daily routines that will lead you to your own pot of gold: your inner treasure.

I am excited for you to start your Career Discovery journey and I want you to know that you are now a part of a sisterhood and a brotherhood of people who have embarked on this same incredible journey. If you stay disciplined and committed to your journey, you will quickly start to see improvements all around you, leading to a more fulfilled life.

Everyone deserves fulfillment and you deserve to have your dreams come true. This is the perfect time for you to step into your own light and discover what you were always meant to do! As your guide, I will walk you through applications that will place you in a direction that will place you on the journey to discover the hidden treasures within you. All you have to do is decide that you will fulfill yourself in all the ways that you want to be fulfilled and TAKE ACTION to follow the callings of your soul. As a start, you can look for ways to feel good each day and I promise that you will find them just as The Alchemist did.

The Alchemist knows that in order to turn anything into gold, you must first have a little bit of gold already. And if you have a little bit of gold that you can place your attention on, then you can wrap your mind in the fact that with time, everything will be 'alchemicalized' around that piece of gold. If you are able to take time to grow into this understanding, you will begin to vibrate at the level of your golden consciousness. It takes only a little bit of belief... a belief the size of a mustard seed. Having a mustard seed amount of faith does not mean having a small amount of faith, you see. The mustard seed knows that it has a mustard tree inside of it! You have greatness inside of you! Start to believe that you are right where you need to be on your path and see how magnificent you are. Have faith and start to dream bigger. Place your attention on where your attention should be. See what is real. See yourself in a brand new lens. Perfect just as you are in this moment. Release fear and self-doubt and start to walk in your truth that is your brilliance.

I welcome you to your journey, to your new mindset and to this opportunity to discover the inner treasure within.

Wrapping you in love and light!

Calling You to Your Greatness

"Our deepest fear is not that we are inadequate. Our deepest fear is that we are powerful beyond measure. It is not our light, but our darkness, that most frightens us. Your playing small does not serve the world. There is nothing enlightened about shrinking so that other people won't feel insecure around you. We are all meant to shine as children do. It's not just in some of us; it's in everyone. As we let our own lights shine, we unconsciously give other people permission to do the same. As we are liberated from our own fear, our presence automatically liberates others."

–Nelson Mandela

This is a guide created for anyone who feels off track, that there is more to life. To the one who may feel lost, afraid, alone, or unfulfilled. This guide is for the graduate student who is unclear of his or her career path. For the young adult who is confused about what his or her life's purpose is. To the one who needs to know that there is more to life than what the eyes see. This guide was created for the truth seeker - anyone looking to connect to his or her higher self and operate at full capacity.

This guide is designed to inspire hope and to open your eyes to new possibilities of what your life can become. It is designed to align your passions with purpose in order to connect you back to the soul of who you truly are. A soul that knows that it is light. A soul that knows that it has purpose. A soul that is ready to dream once again.

This guide is designed to prove that you truly can bring your dreams to life. All you have to do is decide that you are ready for change and develop new daily routines. To do more in this world, you must first become more. This guide will assist you to connect to your life's calling and position you to discover what you are meant to do while here on earth.

You are being called to your greatness because there is an inner light within you. There is an inner space in which you dwell that is the best version of who you are. There is an inner being that is your higher self. Your higher self is the space where the light of who you are exists and is the person that the world needs to meet. It is from this space that you will create all that you were born to do. It is from this space that you will allow the Spirit of who you truly are to be set free.

Neurolinguistic Programming (NLP) techniques, brain strengthening and training, life visioning, career mapping, mindfulness, and metaphysical methodologies are infused throughout this guide you to help you in discovering what you were always meant to do. Plan to embark on this journey by devoting at minimum one hour each day to do the work in this guide and pace yourself, as you feel comfortable.

This guide is at the intersection of metaphysical science and business strategy and is composed of three parts: Mental Optimization, Passion and Purpose Alignment, and the Career Discovery Journey.

Part 1: Mental Optimization

Before focusing on your passions, purpose, and business, we need to do some housekeeping on interpersonal components to ensure that you are operating at your highest potential. In this section, you will learn tools designed to expand the neuroplasticity in your brain so that you can utilize more brain power. Being able to utilize more brain-power means that you will be limitless in what you accomplish.

This section will guide you to:

- Learn your top five strengths
- Learn the power of affirmations (I AM Statements)
- Understand why you need to have more fun, according to science
- Learn meditation techniques and gain an understanding of how this daily practice will benefit you
- Activate your brain's pineal gland
- Release stress through your body's energy centers (your chakras)
- Understand what you are attracting into your life
- Learn to read vibes/energy
- Develop morning rituals
- Break free from mental conditioning

Part 2: Passion and Purpose Alignment

After working to strengthen your brain's power and develop mental optimization, you will then align your passions with purpose.

In this section, you will move forward in your journey and learn:

- What your passions are by completing a Passion Assessment
- How you can become a voice of hope to inspire others

Part 3: Career Discovery

After you have aligned your passions with purpose, it will be time to bring your journey full circle to learn how to monetize your talent.

In this section, you will:

- Start to map out your career path
- Understand the power of vision boards
- Discover your purpose
- Develop self-mastery
- Follow your inner guidance system
- Develop a Millionaire's Mindset
- Learn the Science of Getting Rich
- Learn to manifest what you want
- Build a business model to create a plan to make money doing what you love

This guide will challenge you to be focused, disciplined, and dedicated. Your journey will ask much of you. It will ask you to open space in your schedule to, once and for all, prioritize yourself. It will ask you to put yourself at the top of your "to-do list." It will guide you through a real life interpersonal scavenger hunt, forcing you to decide to either continue on the same unfulfilling path that you are on now or to finally embrace that nudging pull that you feel at the core of who you are, where all of your hopes, desires, and dreams reside. My hope is that you will choose the latter option.

The way this guide works is simple. You will complete various daily activities that are all designed to pull out the best of who you are. Activities that are suggested are backed by scientific case studies, context, and information to ground your knowledge of understanding and build your comfort level. The time commitment is something to highlight here. Once you decide that you want to break free from robotic routines and start to live life on your own terms, you will commit to at minimum, one hour a day, to invest in your future self.

Furthermore, know that this guide is designed as a self-paced journey. You get to complete "APPLICATION processes" after each section of this guide. Be encouraged to take your time completing the application processes, as this is how you tap into the hidden treasures within you. The applications after each chapter are designed to unlock your inner guidance system. Think of it as doing a scavenger hunt, only the treasure is hidden deep within you and unlocking your inner treasure is what this journey is all about.

Follow the great mystery, one clue at a time! Allow yourself to unfold, embrace the process, and always, trust yourself and your journey.

You're not going to master
the rest of your life in
one day. Just relax.
Master the day. Then keep
doing that every day.

Part 1:

Mental Optimization

According to the Substance Abuse and Mental Health Services Administration (SAMHSA), 43 million Americans have a mental health condition and 56% of American Adults with a mental illness do not receive treatment. This means that 1 in 4 American adults are affected by a mental health problem per year. The reality is that mental health affects us all. The good news is that we can strengthen our mind by learning and practicing mental optimization techniques.

In an article written in October 2015 entitled "Brain Optimization Secrets", Gilbert Ross wrote:

> "Your mind can easily work 'sub-optimally' in adverse conditions, and it's no surprise that it's often the case. Think about a situation where you felt a real good mental performance – you were focused, had clear thoughts, could remember things in a flash and creative solutions were flowing in easily. Now compare that to a time when your thoughts were foggy, found it hard to concentrate for more than a few minutes, got stuck for words or names and felt mentally

drained in general. That's the difference between a healthy brain functioning optimally and one that is not."

In order to develop more brain power, it is necessary to exercise the mind just as you would strengthen any other muscle in your body. Brain care techniques are designed to expand your neuroplasticity and achieve mental optimization. In the first part of this guide, you will learn techniques designed for you to leverage your strengths, intentionally have more fun, learn to meditate (or build upon your meditation practice if this is something you already do), and strengthen your pineal gland. You will also learn to release toxic behaviors, which are detrimental to your mental health, and you will commit to forming positive habits. This entire first section is designed to promote towards healthy brain function.

We are often taught how to care for our bodies and how to eat right but rarely are we taught techniques to care for our minds. Mental Optimization will be the first focus so that you know how to mentally recharge yourself as often as you need to.

To get started, let's discover your first treasure: your inner strengths.

Rise and Shine

CHAPTER 1

Strength's Finder

"Still I rise." –Maya Angelou

Have you ever seen a sales graph? If so, you'll notice that oftentimes, people look at the graph, they follow the line of progress and they notice a large dip on the path. That dip represents a time when something went severely wrong. That dip usually represents inadequacy, a shortcoming, and a time where failure was present and clearly sales were lost. Typically, in a dip, everyone's attention is focused on what went wrong and a lot of negative energy is created at that moment. It doesn't feel good when things go wrong. It is for that reason that I don't like focusing on dips.

I look at a graph, follow the line, and find the spikes! I like to focus all attention on what went right and then replicate that! This approach is called Appreciative Inquiry (AI), which revolutionized the field of organization studies and the strengths based movement in American management. Appreciative Inquiry teaches us to find the best in all situations. To wire your brain to learn how to focus on your strengths and not on your weaknesses, you will first learn what your strengths are.

The first activity that I ask each mentee of mine to do is to purchase Strength's Finder 2.0 by Tom Rath. Strength's Finder, similar to Appreciative Inquiry, teaches you to focus and play to your strengths. You will become so excited to learn your strengths, that you may (like me), also recommend this book to everyone you know. So believe it or not, I am going to ask you to take a day or two off from reading this guide, and pause, to learn your strengths.

Finding your inner treasure within start here. Your first assignment is to purchase Strength's Finder 2.0.

Read the first part of the book (when I read it, the first part was only 30 pages and it took me 2 hours to read). Then you will take the assessment that the Strength's Finder book provides to learn what your Top 5 Strengths are.

After you complete the assessment, you will return to this guide and complete your first application below.

APPLICATION 1: Reflect on your Top 5 Strengths

- How did learning about your strengths make you feel?

  _____

  _____

  _____

  _____

  _____

- How can you incorporate your strengths into your life today?

  _____

  _____

  _____

  _____

  _____

_____

_____

_____

_____

_____

- What else did you learn about yourself?

_____

_____

_____

_____

_____

- How are you feeling about yourself now that you have completed this part of your journey?

_____

_____

_____

_____

_____

Pause from reading until you have completed your first application.

Application Notes

Application Notes

Application Notes

Evolve, Uplift,
Succeed, Repeat!

CHAPTER 2

Neurolinguistic Programming - "I AM" Statements

"Be still and know that I AM God."

A mind is a powerful tool. It can work for you or it can work against you if you allow it to.

The thoughts that we have about ourselves, our work, and our life can set the tone of all that we do. If you allow yourself to have negative thoughts, you are allowing your mind to operate in a space of toxicity. Each negative thought is the equivalent to a weed that is being placed in your mental garden, leaving no room for it to flourish and harvest. The mind is an amazing gift full of infinite potential that can work for us if we allow it.

Oftentimes, our thoughts hold us back from designing the life we deserve to have. The beauty in this is that we have control over our thoughts. You may have heard that *thoughts become things*. What you think about yourself matters and if you have negative thoughts, it is now time to release what is not serving you. What would it mean to you to free yourself and restore happiness in your life? What would it change? Lucky us, science offers us a method called Neurolinguistic Programming (NLP) that we can use to our advantage to overcome negative thought patterns.

According to Wikipedia, **Neuro-linguistic programming (NLP)** is "An approach to communication, personal development, and psychotherapy created by Richard Bandler and John Grinder in California, United States in the 1970s. NLP's creators claim there is a connection between neurological processes (*neuro-*), language (*linguistic*) and behavioral patterns learned through experience (*programming*), and that these can be changed to achieve specific goals in life."

Before learning this technique, I struggled to keep my mind in a positive state. In fact, I struggled with depression for over 20 years of my life. I now use this NLP technique daily to keep my mind in check and to set the tone of my day. The first thing that I do when I wake up is to look at myself in the mirror and program my mind. When I look in the mirror, I first gaze in my eyes and that is how I am able to connect to myself deeper. I then give myself programming treatments. By programming my mind and controlling what information I expose myself to, I am now more balanced, focused, and happier than I've ever been.

To start your NLP process, we will first need to address any self deprecating thought patterns that are holding you back from having the peace and happiness that you are so deserving of. As you progress, you will build upon this Mental Optimization technique and by practicing it daily, you will be in a great position to soon have clarity on what your life's purpose is.

Now is the perfect time for you to begin to walk in your brilliance and become the best version of who you are in order to then start the process of career mapping, which will take place in part three of this guide. For now, lets begin the process and examine your current brain patterns to then release what is not serving you.

What are your thoughts telling you? Is your mind working for or against you? What is holding you back from living the life you deserve? This is a moment for you to show up to honestly self-assess and have some genuine inner dialogue. This is your moment to resolve these thoughts, face them, and correct them once and for all. Take a deep breath before you start this application, be transparent and honest with yourself as you self assess, and continue to breathe deeply throughout this entire process.

APPLICATION 2: Neurolinguistic Programming - "I AM" Statements

- Grab a piece of paper.

- Fold the paper in half, horizontally (the long way).

- On the first column, the left hand side, write I AM at the top of the page. You will create a list of "I AM" statements. Do not go over the line. You may use additional pages to write only on the left hand side. You may use as many pages as you need.

- This is an opportunity for you to purge and release the negative thoughts and leave them here on this paper. Write out what you believe you are in the form of "I AM" statements. For example, if you believe that you are overweight, write, "I AM overweight." If you believe that you are a procrastinator, write, "I AM a procrastinator." Take as much time as you need and sit in the true negative self-deprecating thoughts that occur. Only write negative statements and take this time to purge out all of the negative beliefs that you have held about yourself. Pause from reading to complete this task now.

- After you have the first column complete, I want you to now dig deeper. Likely, what you wrote on this column are thoughts that you share easily. These are thoughts that you will confide in some friends with. These are thoughts you may even share with a therapist. Now, you must write out "I AM" statements and get out the things that you do not feel comfortable talking about. In doing this, know that you are in a safe space. This is your opportunity to mentally detoxify all that is holding you back. Now, what is deep within? Go back to your "I AM" list and extend it on the same column. Pause from reading to complete this step.

- Now that you have the left column of negative "I AM" statements complete, you will use the right side column of your paper to balance the energy by writing the complete opposite statement. For example, if the first line reads, "I AM overweight," you will go to the other side of the paper and write: "I AM healthy," on the right hand column. Go line by line and write positive "I AM" statements on the right hand side of your paper(s). Pause from reading to complete this task now.

- Now that all of your negative "I AM" statements have been balanced to positive statements, it is time to tear/cut the paper down the middle to separate the negative statements from the positive. Place all positive papers on top of each other. Place all negative papers on top of each other. Grab a pair of scissors and a bag. Fold the negative

"I AM" papers and use the scissors to cut the statements into the bag. Cut it into tiny pieces and as you do this do it with the belief that you are releasing all negative, self-deprecating labels from yourself. This bag represents your baggage. Pause from reading to cut the negative statements.

- Now that you have the negative statements in the bag, cut into tiny pieces, look at the bag for a few seconds. This bag represents how the world has known you to be. This is how you showed up to the world. This is who you believed you were. This bag is full lies–false beliefs. This bag is not who you are.

- Reflection: How long have you carried this baggage around? 5 years? More? How does that make you feel? Can we agree that you have suffered enough and that you now deserve to be free from this weight? The world has seen you show up in the energy of this bag; we have yet to see you step into your brilliance.

- Realize that you have the power to free yourself right in this moment!

- Today's Affirmation: I AM FREE

- The energy of the bag now must be released and you must release it before the end of the day (midnight). You can release it into the wind as you drive. You can release it by throwing it into the trash. You can drown it. You can burn it. Decide now how you want to release your baggage.

- Take note that self love in this moment and for the rest of the day is so important. What you are releasing takes so much strength, courage, and energy so give yourself permission to mother yourself today just as you would mother a child. Follow your impulses on what you need to do to recharge your mind, body, and spirit. To assist to recharge, plan to sit in meditation longer this evening to restore yourself. Remind yourself that you are NOT any of the negative experiences that have happened to you. You are not any of the negative labels and names that anyone has ever said to you. You are not any of the negative things that you have done. You are NOT your mistakes. You are not any of the negative beliefs that you have held on to all these years. You are so much more than this and it's time for you to see yourself in a new way.

- You are whole. You are perfect just as you are. You are everything that you wrote on the right side of the paper and it is time that you begin to see yourself in this light. In order to change your mindset, you will use a neurological programming technique to train your mind to view your truth. You are now stepping into your brilliance and when you wake up tomorrow, you will feel so much better. You will feel relaxed, refreshed, and rejuvenated. Tomorrow is a new day and a new day brings a fresh new start for you to enjoy being who you are.

- Now let's move forward to handle more of what needs to be handled. After you release the baggage, hold on to the positive "I AM" statements and plan to read them to yourself while looking into a mirror at the beginning of every day. To set your daily positive energy, I recommend saying your "I AM" statements right after you get out of bed, before you do anything else.

- Go to your local store (or Amazon) and purchase washable markers. Write your statements on your mirror in the bathroom and read them every morning for the next 30 days. This is a great time to unplug from all social media, TV, and any other form of distraction, so that you can focus solely on your healing. After the month is up, you can decide to continue to unplug and use your social media for productive purposes (e.g. inspirational posts, marketing your business, or any other positive social media activity that you can do within five minutes per day). Remember, if you expose yourself to miscellaneous information, you will get miscellaneous results. Now is the time to stay focused on your path and eliminate distractions.

- Reward yourself for what you have just done. Releasing this weight took true strength, and you are handling this like the warrior that you are! After you write your statements on a mirror, set an intention to buy yourself a freedom bracelet. This bracelet will represent the new you and the positive path that you are committing yourself to now walking. As you are out and about shopping, you will see a bracelet that catches your attention. It is waiting for you. Buy it. Wear this bracelet with pride, knowing that you are a beautiful free spirit, perfect... even in your imperfection. Know who you are. Stand firm in your dignity, truth, and power to not allow anything to dim your light.

- Use the "I AM" statement method as often as you'd like to manage negative thought patterns, and continue to create new healthy statements that reflect who you truly are. Any time your mind tells you something negative, immediately say: "cancel, cancel, cancel," and then say the positive opposite statement to yourself. This neurological programming method is a great tool to use to release negative thoughts and transmute them into positive self-serving thoughts as often as you need to.

Pause from reading until you have your positive I AM statements listed on your mirror.

Application Notes

Application Notes

What is your soul
calling you to do?

CHAPTER 3

Why You Need to Have More Fun, According to Science

"When someone told me I lived in fantasy land,
I nearly fell off my unicorn." -Unknown

Google, Facebook, LinkedIn, Apple and almost every other top Fortune 500 company that I can think of has two things: meditation programs and fun centers. We'll discuss meditation and its benefits in an upcoming chapter, but for now, let us keep our focus on having more fun. Google places a high value on their employees' fun experiences so much that they have actual fun centers placed in each building and every employee is encouraged to make fun a priority.

Typically, when we think of FUN, we get uncomfortable because fun is often something that we regard as child's play. It seems like it is not as easy to have fun as it used to be. The reasons why we do not have fun vary between our own guilt and our perceived time of what it would take. Or because we think that the roles and responsibilities that we have won't allow us the time for fun. How cool, then, is it that science gives us the green light to have more fun?

According to the Oxford Dictionary, fun is defined as "amusement, especially lively or playful." If we embrace this definition, we can connect the word to fun things that are enjoyable for us to do and experience. Fun is sometimes used interchangeably with play, and some would argue that play is a state of mind. It is important to stay mindful that what is fun to you might not be fun to others. For this reason, your fun will be activities that only you do for yourself and by yourself.

Lucky us, science has our back! Science gives us five reasons why fun needs to be a priority.

1. Having fun improves your personal and professional relationships.
2. Having fun makes us smarter. Remember, Einstein said, "Creativity is intelligence having fun." What can you create? What can you do to have fun?
3. When we have fun, we reduce stress.
4. When you engage in physical activity, you balance your hormone levels.
5. Fun can make you more energetic and youthful.

Now that we understand that science has our back, let's dig deeper to focus on our own happiness.

As a child, I used to love to color. I used to walk everywhere. I walked almost every day because I loved to be around nature. I remember asking for seventy-five cents as a kid so that I could go down to the community pool, The Plunge, and swim all day. Swimming was definitely on my top ten things to do. The water felt calming and nourishing against my skin. I also remember going to the beach and enjoying how massive the water felt; I loved being in front of an enormous body of water and absorbing the experience of it beneath the warmth of the sun. Riding my bike was also a favorite pastime. I'd do anything just to be outside, which brought me so much happiness. Those still are things that I do for fun to this day. Now, it's your turn! What do you like to do for fun?

Take a few minutes to reflect on your childhood. Think of the positive things only. What did you do as a child for fun? Before you had to earn a paycheck and work a job. Before you had to learn how to be an adult. Before life's demands weighed heavily on your shoulders. What did you do? How did you allow your creativity to express itself? Take a minute and think of ten things that you used to do for fun as a child.

As you write your list below, remember that these are things that are your true passions.

APPLICATION 3: Making Time for More Fun

- List 10 things that you did for fun as a child.

1. _____
2. _____
3. _____
4. _____
5. _____
6. _____
7. _____
8. _____
9. _____
10. _____

- Reflect on these fun activities. How did reflecting on your childhood fun activities make you feel?

  _____

  _____

  _____

  _____

  _____

- How can you incorporate these 10 fun activities back into your life starting today?

  _____

  _____

  _____

  _____

  _____

- What else did you learn about yourself?

  _____

  _____

  _____

  _____

  _____

- How are you feeling about yourself now that you have completed this part of your journey?

  _____

  _____

  _____

  _____

  _____

TAKE ACTION: Schedule happiness into your calendar just as you would any other task for work. Nothing is more important than your happiness and you are responsible for making sure that you maintain it. To start to care for your own happiness, commit to doing one thing on this list for at least one hour a day. Focus on making your happiness a priority and fulfill yourself, as you want to be fulfilled. Know that there is no limit to this list. You can continue to build on this list as your passions unfold.

Guidance: *"Wake up! Remember what excites you! Think of these things, those friends, and the adventures that can be yours! Focus. Care. Fantasize. Imagine. It's all so near. Speak as if you're ready. Paste new pictures in your scrapbook, on your vision board, and around your home and office. Physically prepare for the changes that you wish to experience in your life. You've done this before. You know it works. You're due for an encore. It's time to amaze yourself once again. That is why you are here. And that is why I am here."* The Universe

Pause from reading until you have completed
the Top 10 List of Fun Things

Application Notes

Application Notes

We all deserve to know
who we truly are.

CHAPTER 4

How Mindfulness & Meditation Can Benefit You

"Nothing can harm you as much as your own thoughts unguarded." -Buddha

Apple, Facebook, Google, and Twitter... what do these companies have in common? These companies offer meditation training to their employees. Google, Facebook, LinkedIn, Target, Ford, and many Fortune 500 companies are realizing the benefits of meditation. Companies are seeing significant increases in their bottom line because their employees feel their absolute best with this practice. Meditation builds a cognitive reserve, and these companies understand that caring for the brain is the key to unlocking company-wide success.

Not many people know what Steve Jobs did as his final act on Earth. Jobs believed in the power of meditation so much that in his final act, he gave copies of meditation books to guests at his own funeral: Paramahansa Yogananda's *Autobiography of a Yogi*. Steve Jobs said, "If you just sit and observe, you will see how restless your mind is. If you try to calm it, it makes it worse. But over time, the brain does calm. You simply have to train it and teach it." Simply put, meditation is teaching your brain how to quiet its thoughts.

In the book, *Breaking the Habit of Being Yourself: How to Lose Your Mind and Create a New One*, Dr. Joe Dispenza writes:

> "You will learn that the true purpose of meditation is to get beyond the analytical mind and enter into the subconscious mind so you can make real and permanent changes. If you get up from meditation as the same person who sat down, nothing has happened to you on any level. When you meditate and connect to something greater, you can create and then memorize such coherence between your thoughts and feelings that nothing in your outer reality—no thing, no person, no condition at any place or time—could move you from that level of energy. Now you are mastering your environment, your body, and time."

To go beyond the analytical mind and enter the subconscious mind, you must first understand the basics of meditation.

Understanding the Basics

There are various ways to meditate. To start, know that you can chant, hum, or simply sit in silence. You can close your eyes or keep them open. Finally, know that there are breath-centric meditations as well as mind-clearing meditations –whatever you need at that moment is available to you.

Common Benefits of Meditation

- Increase of focus
- Less anxiety

- Increased creativity
- More compassion for others
- Better memory
- Less stress

Meditation Apps

One of the best apps (and it's free!) to help you get started with meditation is called Headspace, invented by former Buddhist monk Andy Puddicombe and entrepreneur Richard Pierson. This is an amazing meditation tool designed for busy people like you and me. Andy guides you through 10 minutes of simple meditation every day. You don't have to do anything—just sit down, turn on the app, and let Andy's calm voice explain how to approach meditation.

APPLICATION 4: Meditate Daily

- Write down a daily plan to meditate.

_____

_____

_____

_____

_____

- What time each day can you set aside for practice?

_____

_____

_____

_____

- How much time can you commit each day to this practice?

  _____

  _____

  _____

  _____

  _____

- What do you need to do to strengthen your practice?

  _____

  _____

  _____

  _____

  _____

- Feel free to incorporate props: incense, candles, a meditation pillow, a meditation robe and whatever else you would like to use as you practice.

  _____

  _____

  _____

  _____

  _____

- Download a meditation app and learn to anchor your breath. Commit to at least 10 minutes of meditation each day to clear your mind, focus, and recharge.

  _____

  _____

  _____

  _____

  _____

Guidance: *"Meditation brings about an inner peace that clears the way for intuition to direct and guide you. Creative ideas flow forth into the conscious mind and that will elevate you above the problem level of mind allowing you to see yourself clearly. Meditation is a practice; meditation is a daily ritual."* -The Universe

Pause from reading until you have meditated for 10 minutes.

Application Notes

Application Notes

Mind, Heart, & Soul Dialogue

Mind: I'm worried.

Heart: Just relax.

Mind: But, I'm totally lost now.

Heart: Just follow me.

Mind: But you've never been there before.

Heart: Trust me, you'll love it.

Soul: If you two would shut up, I'd show you the map.

CHAPTER 5

Brain Training - Pineal Gland

*"Enlightenment is when a wave realizes it
is the ocean."* –Thich Nhat Hanh

Training your pineal gland is another great way to strengthen your brain's power for mental optimization. According to the Merriam-Webster dictionary, the pineal gland is "a small, typically cone-shaped structure of the brain that arises from the roof of the third ventricle, is enclosed by the pia mater, and functions primarily as an endocrine gland secreting melatonin." The famous philosopher Descartes described the pineal gland as the "principal seat of the soul."

Commonly referred to by ancient cultures and mystics as "***the third eye***," our pineal gland sits in the center of our brain between our right and left hemispheres and is responsible for producing neurotransmitters such as serotonin and melatonin. The pineal gland wasn't bestowed the name "*third eye*" for just any random reason. Rather, when dissected from the brain, it is found that the pineal gland actually contains photoreceptors just like our own two seeing eyes and is actually activated by light transmitted through our two eyes. This sunlight transmitted through our eyes stimulates the pineal gland's production of serotonin and further works to strengthen the gland's ability to break free of specific harmful chemicals that can encrust it. As well, the pineal gland is also stimulated by darkness, in which the gland responds by producing melatonin to help induce us into sleep.

The pineal gland is located in your brain in the middle of your eyebrows. It is a rice-sized, pine cone-shaped organ. How you think and feel every day depends on the pineal gland. It modulates sleep patterns and produces melatonin. This part of your brain should be strengthened just as you would strengthen any other muscle in your body.

*Note that the techniques listed below are optional, should be done responsibly, and avoided if they are uncomfortable in any way.

There are five ways to activate and strengthen the pineal gland:

1. Eat chlorella, spirulina, wheatgrass, oregano oil, apple cider vinegar, and beet juice. Also, eliminate all sources of fluoride since it is known to calcify parts of the brain. This includes toothpaste that has fluoride (use an alternative such as Tom's toothpaste or flavored activated charcoal). Foods like cilantro, garlic, lemon juice, and coconut oil will detoxify the fluoride from your system, and you will also want to avoid junk foods, especially soda.

2. Get out into the sun. Sun exposure kick starts the gland and stimulates your mind. Any type of light exposure will produce serotonin, which is the neurotransmitter responsible for your mood and energy levels.

3. Sleep in complete darkness. A dark environment ensures your pineal gland produces enough melatonin necessary

to enjoy a good and restful sleep. Before you rest, 30 minutes before bed, avoid backlit devices such as phones, tablets, computers, and TV.

4. Meditate. The pineal gland responds to the bioelectric signals of light and dark, and meditation activates this bioelectric energy. With practice, you will learn to direct energy to this highly sensitive organ.

5. Sun gaze. Sun gazing is definitely a controversial exercise but many people, including employees at NASA, practice it and it has been scientifically proven to be the quickest pineal gland activator. Here are the basics of sun gazing:

- Only look at the sun when the sun is orange (during sunrise or sunset).
- Start for only 10 seconds at a time and increase this time gradually.
- Educate yourself further on this technique.

*Note that this information and these statements are for educational purposes and should not replace any doctor's advice.

Since looking at the sunrise or sunset for 10 seconds may not be an option at this moment, you can experience the same benefits and immediately strengthen your pineal gland by looking directly into a candle flame for 10 minutes. This technique works because the sun is a ball of fire just as the lit candle provides a flame of fire. Expose yourself to the fire element daily or as often as you can.

You will learn how to ingest fire and candle gaze as the next application.

APPLICATION 5: Candle Gaze Technique

- Select a time and place in your home where you will not be disturbed. If noisy, use earphones and listen to meditation music while doing this practice.

- Wear loose and comfortable clothing.

- Sit in an upright position at a table or desk with your back and spine as straight as possible.

- Place a single white candle in front of you on the table or desk.

- For approximately 10 minutes, look into the flame of the candle. This is the quickest way to clear your thoughts. Note: you do not have to time yourself.

- After approximately 10 minutes, close your eyes. You will see an afterimage of the candle flame in your mind's eye.

- Concentrate on the afterimage. With most people, the glow fades out after two or three minutes. You are using the afterimage as a focal point of concentration, and this will allow you to have a direct and focused level of inner concentration.

During the moment of inner concentration, after you have focused on using your third eye, you may experience the following:

- Cloud-like formations of color
- Pictures of various phenomena, flat or multi-dimensional
- Images from your subconscious mind

If you do not see an afterglow or an afterimage, that means that your pineal gland is likely calcified and you will need to do the following to decalcify:

- Check that your water and toothpaste does not have fluoride in them. If your toothpaste does, throw it out and use either activated charcoal or Tom's.
- Eat as much watercress, bananas, avocados, and pineapples, as you can daily and also drink coconut water, as these are all natural decalcifiers.
- Continue to sun and candle gaze as a daily practice.

Ingesting fire daily will expand your neuroplasticity, strengthen your pineal gland, and create a sacred time for you to rejuvenate your mind and feel at peace.

Pause from reading until you have your
first sun or candle gaze experience.

Application Notes

Application Notes

Exercise gives us health
of the body; meditation
gives us health of the
mind. Each strengthens
the other. Strong mind.
Strong body. Strong spirit.

CHAPTER 6

Chakras - Understanding the Basics

"Sky above. Earth Below. Peace Within." –Unknown

To understand the chakras, we must first understand the biology of energy. When we move, rest, think, breathe, digest food, repair ourselves and even when we sleep, energy is flowing through our bodies via our neurons and nerve pathways. We can think of the nerve pathways as correlating to the energy rivers that run through our bodies.

Within our autonomic system is a nerve called the Vagus Nerve, which connects the brainstem to the body. This nerve links the neck, heart, lungs, and the abdomen to the brain and connects to the spinal cord at three places. The Vagus Nerve is responsible for counteracting the fight or flight response and switching the body back into rest and digest mode.

The Vagus Nerve corresponds with something that the Hindu scriptures call kundalini. Kundalini is a description of the energy that flows through our body. It is described as a snake that begins at the base of the spine and winds up to the crown of the head coiling three times as it travels up the spine. 'Kundalini awakening' is said to result in enlightenment and a deep sense of bliss.

Luckily, there are many ways in the ancient Hindu tradition to stimulate the kundalini energy. Deep breathing, meditation and yoga are excellent ways to achieve this as are many chakra healing techniques.

I came home from work one day to find my boyfriend meditating through his Chakras. At the time, I was new to meditation; I only knew how to meditate by quieting my thoughts and anchoring my breath. This new type of meditation practice fascinated me, and I spent an entire year studying my chakras, how they store energy, and how I could also learn to meditate through them. This was when I first learned that there are many different ways to meditate to release blocked energy in the body. This is now a practice that I do daily, even if for 10 minutes, in my car, while on my lunch break.

Having blocked energy in any of our chakras can lead to an imbalance in our body and can result in illness if not cleared out. Many ancient religions have understood that the movement of this energy is an essential part of our health, and existence. Many energy healing practices, such as Reiki, Qi Gong, Yoga, Tai Chi, and Chakra Healing, focus on manipulating this energy in order to restore harmony and well-being.

According to Kemetic Law, we have many chakras, which operate as energy centers throughout our bodies. I am going to focus on the seven main chakras, which follow the spine from the base of the backbone to just above the crown of the head. The seven chakras along the spine are the root, sacral, solar plexus, heart, throat, third eye, and crown. With this in mind, it is important to understand what each chakra represents and what we can do to keep the energy flowing freely at each level.

1. The Root Chakra is located at the base spine in our tailbone area. It represents our foundation and our ability to feel grounded. When you experience emotional issues relating to your survival, finances, independence, money or food, you will want to meditate focusing your attention at the Root Chakra to clear out the imbalance.

2. The Sacral Chakra is located at the lower abdomen about two inches below the navel. It represents our ability to accept others and new experiences. When you experience difficulty with abundance, your well-being, pleasure, and sexuality, you'll want to focus attention here in your meditation practice.

3. The Solar Plexus Chakra is located in your upper abdomen in the stomach area. It represents our ability to be confident and in control of our lives. If ever your self-worth, confidence, and self-esteem become challenged, this is where you can focus your attention.

4. The Heart Chakra is located at the center of our chest just above the heart. It represents our ability to love. When you struggle with love, joy, or inner peace, this is where you can heal those areas.

5. The Throat Chakra is located at the throat. It represents our ability to communicate. If communication or self-expression of feelings and truth become an issue, this is where you will focus.

6. The Third Eye Chakra is located between our eyes. It represents our ability to focus on the big picture. If you experience emotional issues with intuition, imagination,

wisdom, and the ability to think and make decisions, this is where you will focus your meditation.

7. The Crown Chakra is located at the very top of our head. It represents our ability to be fully connected spiritually. When you struggle with your inner and outer beauty, or your connection to spirituality, you can clear out the imbalance and center yourself back to pure bliss, which is your true natural state of being.

Now that we have a foundational understanding of our seven chakras, what they represent and the emotional areas that they are tied to, we have the power to control our energy at each level. In meditation, stay focused on how you feel and learn to meditate through your chakras to support your health and happiness.

APPLICATION 6: Body Scan

- Based on the chakra information above, close your eyes and scan your body from head to toe. Feel each inch of your body. Each cheek. Feel your shoulders. Feel your upper back. Your chest. Do you feel any type of tightness in or tension in these areas? If so, locate that area and identify the tension where the chakra is blocked from storing energy. What area in your body needs your immediate attention?

  _____

  _____

  _____

  _____

  _____

- Take 10 minutes to practice meditating through your chakras.

Guidance: *"It's working! Every day you are getting closer! Everything you've ever wanted is being pressed toward you. Everything is clicking. Don't let the illusions trick you. Don't let the events of today dampen your spirits. Things couldn't be any better than they are now. You couldn't have more reasons to celebrate. Continue! Press on! The hardest work is done! Keep showing up, be present, open every door and let events unfold. Life is your stage. This is your paradise. Together, we can do anything. I love it when you're hot." –The Universe*

Pause from reading until you have completed
a 10-minute chakra meditation.

Application Notes

_____

_____

_____

_____

_____

_____

_____

_____

_____

_____

_____

_____

_____

_____

Application Notes

_____

_____

_____

_____

_____

_____

_____

_____

_____

_____

_____

_____

_____

_____

My insight is stronger
than my eyesight.

CHAPTER 7

Understand What You Are Attracting Into Your Life

"That, which you are seeking, is seeking you." –Rumi

Now that you have completed a chakra meditation, you can use this interchangeably with your other meditation practices based on what you feel you need. Think of this as adding to your own personal toolbox of things to do each day to feel your best and to activate The Law of Attraction.

According to the New Thought philosophy, the Law of Attraction is the belief that positive or negative thoughts bring positive or negative experiences into a person's life. The Law of Attraction in motion is the ability to attract whatever it is you are focused on. If you focus on the good, you will attract more good. If you focus on negativity, you will attract more negativity. Think about what you place attention on from day to day and from moment to moment. To monitor your thought patterns, you can use a technique called Invisible Boxes. Picture having two boxes that you can place a thought into. One box is useful and the other box is not useful. Place each thought that you have into a box to train your mind to focus on positivity. Do not think about what you do not want to experience. Train your mind to focus on things that feel good to you to positively activate the Law of Attraction.

Do you often notice how people have wronged you? Do you find yourself in toxic situations? Do you find yourself in conflict with other people? If you answered yes to any of these questions, then you are likely attracting more of these toxic, dramatic, and hurtful experiences into your life. This Universal Law, The Law of Attraction, is absolute and it will give you more of what you focus on. If you say that you are always running late, then you will find that to be true. If you say that you are disorganized, then so it is. Even if you say that you don't want any more car issues, the Universe hears "car issues" and you will find yourself having this experience as often as you say it. If you say that you don't have enough money, a lack of money will be your reality. You must stay mindful of your words and focus solely on what you want. Do not focus on what you do not want. The key to understanding this is that your words have power and they create your reality.

People who have good emotional health are aware of their thoughts, feelings, and behaviors. Negative energy is lethal to your mind, body, and soul and will work against your intentions if you focus attention on it. The good news is that you have control over what you experience. All you have to do is make a decision on what you will focus on and what you will not focus on and become a vibrational match to that which you want to attract into your life. The words you use are that powerful!

In order to properly align your passions with purpose, you must become a ***vibrational match*** for that which you seek. Meaning, you must be in full mind, body, and spirit alignment with who you are to have full clarity around your life's calling. You cannot have full clarity until you are able to release dead weight, baggage, and toxic behaviors and unhealthy relationships in order to allow new positive habits to flow. Negative emotions affect your overall physique.

In 2004, Dr. Masaru Emoto presented a water experiment where the energy of thoughts and words are demonstrated. In his central premise, he proposed that people can affect the shape and molecular structure of water simply by conscious intention. He demonstrated this premise in two ways. He first showed images of water molecules from the Fujiwara Dam before and after a monk had blessed them. Then he showed the impact of labeling bottles of distilled water with positive and negative words. He froze the contents from each bottle and photographed them at sub-zero temperatures using a high-powered microscope camera. The results were astonishing.

The resulting shape, color, and structure from the water crystals showed distinct variations. Water from the positively labeled bottle contained shiny, diamond-like beautiful qualities. Those that were labeled with negative thoughts froze with deformed, collapsed structures with black holes and distorted edges.

The water bottle study is significant. If labeling bottles with negative words can have such damaging results, what do you think happens when you expose yourself to negative thought patterns? Your body is made up of 70% water. If negative emotions influence a bottle of water to this extent, imagine what the impact is on your body.

In order to fulfill your purpose, you must be willing to release negativity on all levels. The next few sections of this guide will focus on releasing negative thoughts, emotions, and behaviors in order to make room for healthy and positive thoughts, emotions and behaviors. By forming healthy patterns, you will experience a healthier lifestyle. You will correct these patterns in order to live a long, healthy, and prosperous life and successfully make an impact on millions of lives. You will correct these patterns in order to align yourself on the positive side of The Law of Attraction and become a ***positive vibrational match*** with that which you seek.

In order to have full mind-body-soul alignment and discover your purpose, commit to eliminating all forms of toxicity in your life by developing healthy habits. The rule of thumb is to give your brain positive things to observe to develop a mindset of gratitude.

To eliminate toxicity and promote positivity in your life, there are 10 healthy habits that you can practice immediately.

1. Change your mindset and welcome all of your experiences knowing that there is a lesson to be learned in all that you do.

2. Unplug from TV and social media. It is easy to let technology absorb our time and distract us from what we are meant to do. Facebook, Instagram, and social media updates are time-wasters that have nothing beneficial to offer. When you expose yourself to miscellaneous information, you get miscellaneous results, which is counterproductive. If unplugging completely is a challenge for you at first, start with 30 days, then go from there.

3. Practice gratitude. Practicing gratitude rewires your brain and positions it to focus on things that feel good. You can create a gratitude journal and commit to writing in it for five minutes before bed, or you can decide to write when you first wake up. Every day, list three things you

are grateful for that are happening in your life right now, and allow yourself to feel the appreciation for those things daily. The key is to develop this habit and to stay in this feeling all the time.

4. Believe in yourself. Do not allow the dogma, opinions of others, or your own mind (when it is not rooting for you) to hold you back from creating the life that you deserve. Instead of focusing on how you are going to get things done, believe that you can get things done and focus on why you want to accomplish something. When you focus on WHY you want something done versus HOW to do it, you become an instant vibrational match for the desires of your heart, making attaining it a thing that feels good. When you focus on HOW you are going to do it, you will start to feel tension and angst and this will not move you forward. Simply focus on your WHY, and do as much as you can within the 24 hours that you are given. Start one day, focus on the day, and do that over and over. If you make this a habit, you will land exactly where you want to be. Henry Ford once said, "Whether you think you can, or you think you can't – you're right." Believe that you can do the things you are being called to accomplish and you will do them!

5. Make happiness a habit, not an end goal. Do not strive for happiness; just decide each day, moment by moment, to simply be happy. Happiness is a choice. Look for things that make you feel good and you will find them. Allow your inner guidance system to work to your benefit. Follow the impulses that feel good and denounce and stay away from anything that feels bad. Stay in your happy bubble and don't let anything or anyone steer you out

of this state. When you find yourself out of alignment, simply take a breath, use your tools, practice gratitude, and move forward. Life is an adventure designed to be enjoyed, and you deserve to feel and experience all of the happiness that your heart desires.

6. Do one small thing every day that makes you feel good. Prioritize self-care and self-love and schedule time each day, even if for one hour, to do the things you love to do. If you love books, read. If you love music, play it and dance your heart out. If you like to be physically active, go for a nature walk or a hike. If you love to write, decide to write every day.

7. Replace the thought that "I cannot do this right now" with "why not?" When procrastination starts to stray, consider what is behind the procrastination. If your body is tired, allow yourself to rest, and then come back to your work and goals when you feel refreshed. Stay mindful about what is hiding behind your procrastination, and the next time you feel like procrastinating, ask yourself honestly where the resistance is coming from. From there, you will be able to do something to alleviate the procrastination.

8. Don't waste time talking to toxic people. You know who these people are: the ones that always have something negative to say, the ones that will be quick to point out what is wrong with you, life, what you are creating, and anything else their negativity can detect. These people are not your tribe. People will either add value to your life or they will subtract and divide. There is no in-between. Choose people who feel like the sun. Choose people who

make you feel 10 feet tall. Choose people who are rooting for you and want to see you win. Remember, you are the sum of the five people that you surround yourself with, so choose wisely.

9. Release any negative feelings, including anger and resentment. Disappointment and feeling wronged in some way are normal parts of life. The feeling is inevitable. But allowing yourself to stay in a negative space will only knock you out of alignment. Instead of focusing on the negative, focus on the things and people that feel good. Develop a positive attitude towards your mistakes and learn to forgive yourself. Making mistakes is a normal part of life and how you approach them matters greatly. Instead of focusing on the mistake itself, try a different strategy of viewing your past by forgiving yourself for the mistakes that you've made. Reflect on your choices, and make a better choice next time in that situation. It's as simple as that!

10. Embrace your best inner self. Instead of being overly critical about everything you do or everything you feel you did wrong, look at yourself through the lens of the best version of who you are: your higher self. You know who that is. It's the version of you who knows the right action to take, the right path, what needs to be done, and which goals need to be pursued. Always keep a conversation going between the self that you currently are and your ideal self, and when in doubt, choose the path of righteousness.

APPLICATION 7: Graph of Highs and Lows

- Grab a piece of paper.

- Draw a timeline graph of the highs and lows of your life. Start by drawing a straight line to signify your birth. Go above your line to spike the line representing high points of your life. Go below your starting line point to represent low points of your life.

- What are the themes that you notice?

  _____

  _____

  _____

  _____

  _____

- What do you need to let go of?

  _____

  _____

  _____

  _____

  _____

- Take time to reflect on the things that do not feel good and write them.

  _____

  _____

  _____

  _____

  _____

- You need to release the things that do not feel good. After you have identified them, decide to forgive yourself for carrying around this weight in the form of these heavy feelings all this time. How many years have you been carrying this around?

- Make a vow to yourself to now move forward with the best intentions for yourself. Learn to be gentle with yourself. You are a home to a life. You are a living and breathing being. You are a cherished memory to someone. You are perfect just as you are, even in your imperfection.

- Fall back in love with who you are and extend more grace to yourself.

- To forgive yourself and others, try this powerful forgiveness technique.

The forgiveness technique has a funny sounding name: Ho'oponopono (pronounced ho-oh-pono-pono). This ancient Hawaiian practice of reconciliation means, "to make right" and has evolved into a modern day tool accessible to all. The basic idea is to take 100% responsibility for everything that's going on in our lives. And here lies the good news and the bad news: we can't blame anyone else anymore (darn it!). On the other hand, we start to take our own power back.

It goes like this:

- I am sorry for the part in me that is causing this.
- Please forgive me.
- I love you. I love you and I love myself.
- Thank you. Thank you for being willing to show me what I need to heal in myself and thank you God/Universe/ Source for dissolving this.

The more you can really feel this prayer, the more powerful it is.

Guidance: *"For simply giving thanks, when you lie down to sleep each night or from time to time, for no reason or no rhyme, you'll begin to move with life instead of against it. You'll be shown that life could not possibly be more beautiful than it already is. You'll see that you are the fountainhead of your experience. You'll remember that you transcend all things time and space, and thus are their very master. And you'll find that you live in a paradise where the only thing that truly seems impossible is how powerful you really are and how much you are loved. What else would you think about, anyway?" –The Universe*

> Pause from reading until you have clarity on what
> negative patterns need to be corrected and until you
> have completed the Forgiveness Technique.

Application Notes

_____

_____

_____

_____

_____

_____

_____

_____

_____

_____

_____

_____

_____

_____

_____

_____

Application Notes

What is the greatest lesson
a woman should learn?
That since day one, she's
already had everything
she needs within herself.
It's the world that
convinced her that she
did not. —Rupi Kaur

CHAPTER 8

Why Does Energy Matter?

"Your vibe attracts your tribe." -Unknown

Energy is commonly referred to as "vibes" and it is important to understand why energy matters.

Have you ever walked into a room where you notice that two people just had an argument? Did you notice the tension in the air? Well, that tension you felt is called Energy. Energy is mostly associated with physics and is commonly known as a person's physical or mental powers (meaning each person has the ability to create good energy or bad energy).

Every person has an energy level that they "vibrate" at. Have you ever heard anyone say, "I don't know what it is about that person, but I just don't feel right about him/her?" or "That person gives me bad vibes." What do these phrases and expressions all mean? It means that what they are feeling is valid.

According to Huffington Post writer Pamela Dussault in the article, "The Benefits of Being in a Higher Vibration," she writes: "We all vibrate energetically at a particular frequency. The lower the frequency, the denser your energy is and the heavier your problems seem" (Dussault, 2012).

How can you assess if you are vibrating at a high or low level? The easiest way is to gauge your emotions. How are you feeling? What would you label your feeling as? If you label it as a positive feeling, you are likely vibrating at a high level, and if you label it negatively, you are likely vibrating at a low level. The chart/tool in the following application can assist you further with your vibration and emotion assessment. Use the tool often and start to read energy in yourself and in others.

Now that we've learned how to read our emotion and label it as a high or low vibration, we need to keep in mind that we cannot avoid negative situations. What can you do if you start to vibrate at a low frequency? We are often faced with what Abraham Hicks calls "contrast to happiness," where situations occur that can set us off track emotionally/vibrationally. There is traffic, work meetings, disappointments, etc. that we are faced with during the day. So what do we do if we start to vibrate at a low frequency? You guessed right... meditate! Meditation is not just a practice that can be done in the morning or at night. It is a practice that can be a "go to" as often as needed. Consider meditation as a fix-it tool whenever you need a quick escape. Since meditation is a personal practice, you can do it as long or as short as you need - 5 minutes or less, to an hour or more and anything in between. The key is to meditate daily.

So, what can you do if you start to vibrate at a low frequency? The answer is easy: you use your tools and apply what you have just learned. Build upon this knowledge and make a conscious effort to control the energy around you. And remember, energy starts with you first! As is often said, "Your Vibe Attracts Your Tribe".

Happiness is a choice and you can choose to vibrate highly by incorporating morning rituals to maintain a high level of happiness. We will soon develop your list of morning rituals, but for now, it is important that you practice holding a positive mindset and attitude to allow positive energy to build momentum.

In order to bring forth your desired response and create a better life, you will need to do the work to develop a positive mindset.

The five guidelines for developing a positive mindset are easy to follow.

1. Realize that you damage yourself psychologically when your attitude is not positive, no matter what events or conditions are taking place. You damage yourself by accepting failing thoughts, which become part of your subconscious mind, forming negative thought patterns. These patterns will not relieve the present situation but will compound it, leading to further difficulties in your near future.

2. Develop a positive attitude that does not accept defeat but regroups and adjusts by tuning into the Source of all wisdom that is within.

3. Develop a positive mindset that knows that in spite of any apparent difficulty, your inner wisdom will always direct you towards a way for improvement.

4. Know that your purpose in life has meaning and it is your destiny to fulfill your purpose within your lifetime.

5. Visualize yourself as a winner and use this positive energy as you engage in your daily affairs. Allow the positive

vibrations in your mind and attitude that you are creating to build momentum, and allow this to be your default natural state of being.

Practice these guidelines daily and when necessary, practice them moment by moment.

APPLICATION 8: Practice reading emotions with the I OM therefore I AM Emotional Vibration Chart

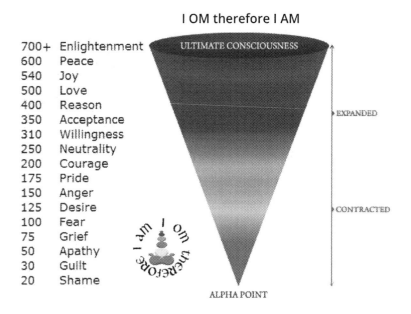

I OM therefore I AM

700+	Enlightenment	ULTIMATE CONSCIOUSNESS
600	Peace	
540	Joy	
500	Love	
400	Reason	
350	Acceptance	EXPANDED
310	Willingness	
250	Neutrality	
200	Courage	
175	Pride	
150	Anger	
125	Desire	CONTRACTED
100	Fear	
75	Grief	
50	Apathy	
30	Guilt	
20	Shame	

ALPHA POINT

- The goal with this chart is to assist you in reading emotions (in yourself and in others) and learn to determine whether you and those around you are vibrating at a high or a low frequency.

- What emotion are you feeling right now and what rate does your emotion have according to the chart?

_____

_____

_____

_____

_____

- Notice the emotion of someone that you recently interacted with. What rate would you give to their emotion?

_____

_____

_____

_____

_____

- The goal with this chart is to stay in a high vibrational level. My goal is to operate at least in a space of Love, which is rated at 500 and is an expanded vibration. When I fall below the expanded level, I meditate until I have balanced back.

- An expanded vibration should always be the default emotional state with Enlightenment being your ultimate goal. When Enlightenment happens, you will know it.

Application Notes

Application Notes

Beautiful is a woman
in alignment with her
divine assignment.

CHAPTER 9

The Importance of Morning Rituals

"Every morning we are born again. What we do today is what matters most." -Buddha

Morning rituals are necessary in order to appropriately set the energy of your day. In order to start your morning rituals, set aside time each day. Consider waking up an hour early to prioritize this time for you.

There are six morning rituals that Steve Jobs, Tony Robbins, Barack Obama, Ellen DeGeneres, Tim Ferris (author of *Tools for Titans*), Bill Gates, Oprah Winfrey, and many other well-known, successful leaders do to kick-start the day.

The best way to remember the flow of the six morning rituals is to remember the **S.A.V.E.R.S.** acronym for silence, affirmations, visualization, exercise, reading, and scribing. Let us examine the six morning rituals further.

1. Silence: There is power in silence. Being able to meditate and sit quietly within yourself for 15-20 minutes each day will position you for great success.

2. Affirmations: Make "I AM statements" daily while looking in the mirror. You can use a washable marker and write your statements on the mirror.

    Consider these affirmations: I am light; I am love; I am safe; I am happy; I am healthy; I am at peace; I am poised; I am open; I am guided; I am abundant; I am positive; I am energetic; I am powerful; I am dynamic; I am the truth; I am whole; I am holy; I am conscious; I am a creator; I am prosperous; I am confident; I am successful; I am full of life; I am the example for others to follow; I am the master of my environment; I am perfection personified; I am radiant; I am brilliant; I am free; I am all that I need; I am perfectly normal; I am light; I am That I am.

3. Visualization: Create a vision board and gaze upon it often so that you stay mindful of what your heart desires. If you do not have a vision board, make it a priority to create one. You will learn more about vision boards in Part 3 of this guide.

4. Exercise: Exercise even if it's a quick 10-15 minute at home yoga mat styled exercise. Prioritize caring for your body and make this ritual non-negotiable.

5. Reading: Franklin Covey encourages us to "sharpen the saw." Set aside at least 10 minutes each day to read to keep your mind (the saw) sharp. Follow your instincts when choosing reading material and lean towards what currently sparks your interest.

6. Scribing: Journal about anything that is in your heart. One exercise that I love to do is to write a letter to God/Source/The Universe.

To do this exercise, simply write "Dear God" at the top of the page and allow whatever is in your heart to flow.

After you get out what you need to say, allow a few minutes to sit quietly. As you sit quietly, you will receive your answer.

After a few moments, write down your answer because that is wisdom and it is coming directly from your inner guidance system. Reflect on this wisdom as often as needed.

Steve Jobs spent his mornings re-evaluating his purpose, work, and desires. In 2005, in his speech to a graduating class at Stanford, Jobs said, "For the past 33 years I have looked in the mirror every morning and asked myself, 'If today were the last day of my life, would I want to do what I am about to do today?' And whenever the answer has been 'No' for too many days in a row, I know I need to change something."

Oprah Winfrey's morning ritual consists of 20 minutes of meditation to clear her mind and set her intentions. Oprah says, "I walked away feeling fuller than when I'd come in. I was full of hope, a sense of contentment, and deep joy. Knowing for sure that even in the daily craziness that bombards us from every direction, there is — still — the constancy of stillness. Only from that space can you create your best work and your best life."

Ellen DeGeneres' morning ritual begins with a workout, followed by 20 minutes of meditation. She believes that her quiet and personal time gives her the energy to carry on with her busy and exciting entertainment schedule.

Tony Robbins calls his empowering morning ritual his "Hour of Power," but sometimes will do "30 Minutes to Thrive" or at least "15 Minutes For Fulfillment." Tony has expressed that a major element of his sustained energy and focus comes from his intense and unusual morning ritual.

Barack Obama starts his morning ritual two hours before any scheduled event or meeting for the day. He starts with a 45-minute workout with weights or doing cardio at his personal gym. Obama says, "The rest of my time will be more productive if you give me my workout time." He also avoids coffee and instead drinks water, orange juice or green tea. And a cardinal rule he also has is avoiding the news or the negativity from his critics.

Bill Gates starts off his morning ritual taking care of his body by spending an hour on the treadmill while feeding his mind by watching courses from the Teaching Company.

If you're not a morning person and want to transform into a creature of the morning, consider these tips:

- Keep your blinds open to let the light in at sunrise. It's harder to get up when it's dark. This obviously doesn't work if your goal is to get up before sunrise, in which case you can turn your light on as soon as your alarm sounds.

- Splash cold water on your face as soon as you wake if you find that refreshing and energizing.

- Take a deep inhalation with peppermint oil under your nose to energize your senses.

- Hop in the shower when you wake up.

- Exercise before you start your workday. Getting endorphins pumping is an effective way to charge your mind and body.

- Don't make giant changes overnight. It won't work if you hate waking up before 10 a.m. and are used to going to bed after 2 a.m. and you try to shift your schedule forward four hours overnight. Move your wake-up time slowly and implement morning rituals incrementally.

- You can use the SAVERS acronym or you can design your own morning routine.

APPLICATION 9: Morning Rituals

- Now it's your turn to develop what your morning routine will be and commit to sticking to it every day.

Here are some more activities that you can consider including in your routine:

1. Read
2. Meditate
3. Exercise/walk
4. Spend time in nature
5. Prepare and eat healthy food
6. Learn how to do breathing exercises and techniques
7. Enjoy a cup of coffee or tea

8. Practice gratitude
9. Write
10. Play music
11. Take time to look your best and enjoy feeling amazing

- My morning rituals are:

  _____

  _____

  _____

  _____

  _____

> Pause from reading until you have
> developed your morning ritual list.

Application Notes

Look at your last 5 text
messages. Are those people
pouring life into you or
are they draining you?

CHAPTER 10

Break Free From Mental Conditioning

"Emancipate yourself from mental slavery.
None but ourselves can free our minds."
–Bob Marley

Okay, I'll admit it; the title of this section may make an eyebrow rise. I get it. I too raised an eyebrow when some of what I had been taught was being challenged. Know that the intent here is not to change your belief system, but to provoke thought.

Let's have a little fun with this. Think of the time that you were taught how to count. It could have been preschool, kindergarten, or at home with your parents and loved ones. If you were raised in a similar upbringing as me, then you were taught to count on a number scale system from 0-9. As we grew older, we learned that numbers are infinite; think of the infinity sign. Just like that!...we are given proof that there was a clear limitation of our learning system and because we were so conditioned to think on a limited basis, we did nothing with knowing that numbers are infinite, yet we only operated on ten of them.

Let's examine this a little further. If numbers are infinite, why were we taught a system of only ten numbers? What could this mean? Well, this valuable insight is proof that mental conditioning occurs. We have been taught to think in tens. We have even been taught that our brains function at 10%. We have been taught to limit our potential.

I was able to break free from mental conditioning because I have always been one to question everything and I love to be challenged. I enjoyed learning new things and understanding that I had the ability to think freely for myself. Being a free thinker feels empowering.

I was always told that I needed to get a "good job" and work hard to climb the ladder in my career. I was taught to work hard for someone else's company and do my best to get a promotion. I was taught to use my skills and talents to build someone else's dream. I was not taught to have my own business and that I could test-drive bigger goals. I was not taught that I could step out of the norm, out of the matrix, and create my own path. When I realized that I could become more than what I was, more than what I had known, I ventured out and created my own company, Career Discovery. Career Discovery empowers you to step into your light and create the life of your dreams. The International Association of Women highlighted my work, and I was honored as their Influencer of the Year in 2018 for my impact in business leadership. Career Discovery is now an international brand creating value for millions of people. Look what can happen when you start to become a free thinker.

So what can you do to start to break free from mental conditioning? A lot.

You can first decide to check your biases and challenge your own thinking. You can then pay attention to your thoughts and learn to use meditation to observe your mind. In doing so, you will develop self-awareness and consciousness. You can further become aware of the effect that certain words have on you and the type of words that generate a strong reaction/feeling for you. Paying attention to words will help you listen more objectively and become less reactive. Finally, you can learn to recognize when your thinking is being corrupted by your ego.

To break free from mental conditioning, you can use the meditative thought below in your next meditation session to unravel the chains of limitation.

APPLICATION 10: Meditative Thought

Meditate on these questions during your next meditation session:

1. Am I happy with the way my life is?
2. What do I need to change in my life right now?
3. Who would I become and what would I do if I were not afraid to fail?
4. What actions can I take to align myself with my purpose?

After you have meditated on the questions, write down new insights you have:

_____

_____

_____

_____

_____

_____

_____

_____

_____

_____

Guidance: *"I understand that you must wonder, sometimes to the point of bewilderment, at what you are truly capable of doing. Yet therein lies the "problem", because living the life of your dreams is far more about what I'm capable of doing. It is time for you to let go and fully surrender." –The Universe*

When you realize that you are full of infinite potential, just as the number system is full of infinite numbers, you too can feel empowered to create the life of your dreams. Build upon this seed and seek out information to learn how to break free from mental conditioning. You can break free and become who you've always meant to be. Step out with courage and into your light.

Pause from reading until you have
completed this meditative thought.

Application Notes

The secret of your
future is hidden in
your daily routine.

Part 2:

Passions & Purpose Alignment

Now that you have worked to develop stronger brainpower for mental optimization, you will now focus on aligning your passions with purpose. Alignment is important because most people feel stressed out, burned out, bored, or frustrated when their talents and skills are not aligned with the work they are doing. Most people strive to use their gifts and share them with the world in a way that feels worthwhile. Most people also get excited about making a positive impact on others and simultaneously doing meaningful work.

Are you doing work that is fulfilling, meaningful, and something that you are passionate about?

It is time to get crystal clear on your passions and how you intend to make the world a better place.

Application Notes

If you want to change
the world, you must
first change yourself.

CHAPTER 11

Discovering Your Passions

*"Allow your passion to become your purpose
and it will become your profession."*
–Gabrielle Bernstein

In the "Path for Greatness," written by Linda Ferguson, she provides a framework for alignment and attaining spiritual greatness. She states, "Personal spiritual greatness comes from having fertile soil (spiritual inspiration, values, and principles), firm roots (purpose), strong stem (passion), developed leaves (gifts), and sweet nectar (service). Your greatness of character, your authenticity, and your integrity blossom out in the magnificence of your being when these are in alignment."

I spent my years from ages 18 to 36 working for Corporate America in sales positions. Eighteen years of my life were spent out of alignment. I was not walking in purpose. I was not living my passions. I was not fulfilled. I was sad, tired, depressed, anxious, and often unhappy. I felt like my dreams were lost. I was unfulfilled and spent a significant amount of my life feeling like there had to be more to life than what I was experiencing. I became tired of being tired and instead of continuing to put a band-aid on my wounds by looking for a resolution in antidepressants, or seeking out the fix to my solutions from external sources, I decided to do the internal work (the SAVERS rituals, eliminating toxicity, forming mental agility, and developing a healthy mindset).

After years of living unfulfilled, I had a breakthrough and began my own journey, which resulted in the applications outlined in this guide. I began my own Career Discovery journey. Two years of deep interpersonal work led me to clarity about my life's purpose, and I am now living my dreams. Creating this guide was a dream. You doing your own inner work and seeing the light that you are is a dream. These dreams came true because I was committed to my process. I did my work and now you must commit to doing your work and do not allow distractions, negativity, or anything else to detour you. You have dreams to actualize!

Feel proud of yourself if you are this far in the book, for you are doing "the work" and you are creating a new life for yourself, the life you deserve.

In order to live a fulfilled life, you must live out your passions. Nelson Mandela said "There is no passion to be found in playing small – in settling for a life that is less than the one that you are capable of living."

Living out your passions is how you live a fulfilled life. In the next application, you will complete exercises to clarify what you are passionate about.

APPLICATION 11: Passion Assessment

Find a quiet place where you won't be disturbed for 30 minutes. Do this exercise on your own, without anyone's input. Write short, clear sentences that answer the following question: "When my life is ideal, I am _____."

Examples:
- When my life is ideal, I am around people that make me feel happy.
- When my life is ideal, I am standing in front of the ocean taking it all in.
- When my life is ideal, I am enjoying perfect health.
- When my life is ideal, I am working with people who share my values.

Write as many statements as you can. Stay mindful that these statements are passions; they are not outcomes (goals). They are the things that get you excited about life.

1. _____
2. _____
3. _____
4. _____
5. _____
6. _____
7. _____
8. _____
9. _____
10. _____

Once you have your list of at least ten things, review your list and take the time to prioritize them. Select the top five priorities and write them below.

1. _____
2. _____
3. _____
4. _____
5. _____

Now rewrite your top five passions in the first person. For example, I enjoy being around people that make me happy. I enjoy bringing my dreams to life. I enjoy being a positive person.

1. _____
2. _____
3. _____
4. _____
5. _____

Write each of your five personal passions as statements on an index card. Place one index card in your car, one by your bed, one in your bathroom, one at work, and other places that you will see daily.

Pause from reading until you have positioned your index cards.

Application Notes

Close your eyes to see
clearly. Be still and you
will hear the truth. —
Ancient Zen Saying

CHAPTER 12

How to Tell Your Story & Become a Voice of Hope

"May your choices reflect your hopes, not your fears." –Nelson Mandela

There is a lot that I like people to know about me. I like people to know that I am a mom. I like them to know that I have worked for Top Fortune 500 companies. I like people to know that I graduated with Beta Gama Sigma honors when I received my masters degree at Pepperdine University. Mainly, I like people to know that I am a success.

What I do not like people to know about me is that I struggled with depression for over 20 years of my life. At one point, I was even suicidal. Trusting others was very difficult for me. I felt alone in this world for many years of my life. I isolated myself because my mind told me that if my mom, the woman who brought me into this world, could give me up, then how could anyone else love me?

I did not like people to know that I was in the foster care system from the ages of 12 to 18. I did not like people to know that I was molested. Things were done to me that I wasn't ready to experience when I was a little girl. I was 13 years old. I wasn't ready to give my innocence up at that age.

There are many things that I do not share and that I do not like people to know about me. Overall, I do not like people to know the dark side of my life.

The truth is I did not know how to cope with trauma so I wore many masks for many years. I was disconnected to the truth of my being and instead of telling my truth, I portrayed that life was perfect. Acting perfect was easier than sharing that I had been hurt. I held in other people's secrets, and that internal toxicity brewing within me started to manifest in my external environment. In the long run, it took a toll. The anger I felt started to manifest in my outer world and it impacted every area of my life. I became someone that I didn't like: an angry woman with a raging temper.

I did everything I thought would help: anger management, therapy, group sessions, I even tried antidepressants. It wasn't until I started to meditate and allow myself to sit in my emotions that I began my journey of healing and self-realization. In meditation, I realized that I was not broken. I realized that I am not any of my negative experiences. I am not the mistake that others have made and I am not the mistake that I have made. I am so much more than that! As I continue to grow into the woman that I am becoming, I no longer feel shame for things that I have endured. I do not feel shame for the darkness that was in someone else.

Healing is something that I do day by day and on some days, it is something I have to do moment by moment. What is liberating is that as each day passes, I am taking my power back and I am starting to openly share my stories because despite it all, I am proud of who I am. I am a survivor. I believe that if I can share my story, I know that we can all share our stories. I now stand tall in my truth and I embrace the life that I have been blessed with. I now use my stories to uplift those who are going through the same things that I overcame. My stories are not mine any longer. They belong to those who need to start their journey of healing. My stories now belong to those who are going through hardships and need to know that they are not alone. I am proud of my stories because they all shaped me into who I am today.

Now, lets put some focus on your stories. Think about what you had to overcome in your life. Go back to the hardest moment that you tried so long to escape from and that you kept secret for so long. Go back to the events that you do not discuss; to the time that caused you to not trust anyone. Go back to the moment that made you believe that you did not matter. Go back to the moment that almost made your spirit break. Hold that moment in your mind for a moment and reflect deeply. What was the hardest thing that you went through? What path did these experiences lead you to? What beliefs did you develop about yourself due to these toxic experiences? Did these moments harden your heart? Did you develop bad behaviors because of it? What did the toxicity look like?

Now that you have the moment in mind, I want you to know that you are strong. Look at what you overcame! Look at how far you've come in your life. What can be learned from these experiences? What good can you pull from having overcome these experiences? How can you change the narrative of these stories to rise victorious?

I am so proud of your victory because you overcame something that did not break you or your spirit. The only thing that these moments did was give you purpose and I will tell you why.

We all have a story. I have a story. You have a story. We all had traumatic experiences and had to overcome some type of adversity in our life. Not everyone makes it out of the darkness. Some people become statistics. Some have turned to drugs and alcohol to cope with the pain. Some took their lives. But look at you... rising in victory above it all.

What would happen if people that were in similar emotional pain came across someone like you? Someone who could inspire hope? Someone who had the power to uplift and stand on the story to use it to empower? What positive words could you share to make an impact and serve as a voice of hope to those who desperately need to know that there is a brighter day ahead?

The beauty of your adversity and your traumatic experiences and stories are that they are no longer your experiences. These moments are no longer yours to hold onto. These experiences and stories had to happen so that you can use them to empower those in need. Your stories now belong to the world because someone needs to hear them and be uplifted from the darkness into the light. Realize that you can stand tall in strength, become a voice of hope, and share your stories with those who need to see an example of what strength looks like. You have the power to make an impact. Realize that your purpose is in your personal story. If not, then why did it happen? When you flip the narrative into a positive use and uplift those who need you, you transmute negativity and rise even higher.

Your story is no longer yours to hold onto. It belongs to those who need to know that life gets better. It belongs to those who need to know that they are not any of the negative things that they have been through. It is now your turn to step into your light, step into your calling, and step out with the courage to strengthen those who need you.

APPLICATION 12: Become a Voice to Inspire Hope

"Sharing your story is a beautiful act of love requiring courage and strength. Hold your head high. Speak even if your voice shakes. Gift your story away in truth and in grace. Each time you tell your story, you will heal more deeply. As you more deeply heal, you will help others to heal more deeply as well. And each time a woman heals, it has a rippling effect. We start to heal a sacred part of the world, which is a sacred part within each one of us." -Jessie Lynn

- What story do you need to tell?

  _____

  _____

  _____

  _____

  _____

- How can you take steps to begin to share your stories?

  _____

  _____

  _____

  _____

  _____

- Who is it that needs to hear your stories?

  _____

  _____

  _____

  _____

  _____

- How will learning about your story help someone else?

  _____

  _____

  _____

  _____

  _____

- What action can you take now to share a story?

  _____

  _____

  _____

  _____

  _____

Guidance: *"I bet you could do something for someone today, who'd remember it for the rest of their life. In a good way. On your mark, get set...." –The Universe*

Pause from reading until you have completed this journal entry.

Application Notes

When you have the
courage to allow your
gifts to be seen, you tap
into your purpose and
everything starts to
line up to serve you.
Put yourself out there;
the world is darker
without your light.

CHAPTER 13

Life Visioning

*"The biggest adventure you can ever take
is to live the life of your dreams."*
—Oprah Winfrey

Have you ever heard the quote, "What you focus on expands?" If you really think about the foundational meaning of this quote, you will see that it is attached to the Law of Attraction. According to Rhonda Byrne, the co-creator and Executive Producer of "The Secret," the Law of Attraction is forming your entire life, moment by moment. When you visualize exactly what you want, you are emitting a powerful frequency, signaling to The Universe.

In a 2017 Forbes article by Bhali Gill titled, "New to Visualization, Here are 5 Steps to Get You Started", Gill encourages us to do the following:

1. Know what you want
2. Describe your vision in detail
3. Start visualizing and create positive emotions around your wants
4. Take daily actions to move towards your goals
5. Have grit and persevere

Gill explains that grit and perseverance are important because you will be faced with many challenges when you set out to create the life that you want. Visualizations will be accountability tools and constant reminders of what you truly want. As you visualize and apply the five steps above, you will start to see your life align with the desires of your heart.

Vision Boards are a physical representation of what you want. Focusing on what you want every single day not only keeps you mindful of what you are working towards, it becomes a sacred representation of what you want out of life. Visualization is one of the most powerful exercises you can do each day.

Oprah Winfrey, Katy Perry, Ellen DeGeneres, Will Smith, and many other successful people have used this method to create the lifestyle they want. I personally have used Jack Canfield's vision board kit, and I make adjustments to my board as my dreams actualize.

You can do the same and find inspiration around you everywhere in determining what you want. You can pull inspiration from magazines, even from websites that inspire you. If you go to Pinterest and type "vision boards", you will see examples of vision boards and also receive helpful tips on how you can create your own. Search "vision boards" on YouTube to tips on creating and using one.

APPLICATION 13: Create a Vision Board

- Use Google to search vision boards and get inspiration.

- Use YouTube to learn how to create a vision board.

- Consider using Jack Canfield's vision board kit to get started (visit http://jackcanfield.com/blog/products/vision-board-collection)

- Collect magazines and cut out statements and images that best reflect what your end represents.

Guidance: *"Better to try and fail than forever wonder what might have been. Not that there's really any failing, because in the journey you will love and be loved, get nearer your goal, and probably realize that you should have dreamed bigger to begin with, as you pluck that baby from the tree of life on a subsequent go around. Tallyho!"* – The Universe

Pause from reading until your Vision Board is complete.

Application Notes

Application Notes

Set your life on fire
and surround yourself
with people who
fan your flame.

Part 3:

Career Discovery

Career Discovery was designed for you to activate your highest potential to create the life that you deserve. Now that you are developing mental optimization and starting to embrace living out your passions, it is time to bring your experience full circle and start dreaming even bigger as you continue on your Career Discovery Journey.

Application Notes

_____

_____

_____

_____

_____

_____

_____

_____

_____

_____

_____

_____

_____

_____

Build your own dream
or someone will hire
you to build theirs.

CHAPTER 14

Career Mapping

"It's never too late to be what you might have been." –Unknown

In the article, *It Pays to Plan* written by Carol Milano, she offers the following advice:

> "The traditional path—graduate school to postdoc to academic tenure-track—is no longer a sure thing. How can you gain an edge in the increasingly competitive world? Start building your career plan. "A body of research shows that people who take the more deliberative approach of setting goals have a better likelihood of meeting them," observes **Jennifer Hobin**, Ph.D., Director of Science Policy at the Federation of American Societies for Experimental Biology (FASEB). That deliberative approach is a career plan: a roadmap guiding you from where you are now to where you'd like to be in one, five, or even ten years. This personal map, or "individual development plan" (IDP), evolves through thoughtful self-discovery. Take time to reflect. Explore your talents, wishes, and realistic opportunities. Creating your IDP will gradually identify professional development needs

and career objectives, and pinpoint milestones along the way to each goal."

It wasn't until I turned 35 that I did my career map. I decided to map out where I wanted to go in life because I was not fulfilled with the work that I was doing. I was working tirelessly for someone else and I was burnt out. I kept feeling a nudging pull inside telling me that I had more to offer this world. This nudging pull was right. When I finally did my career map, I landed right where I am… doing what I love.

Where do you want to go in life and how to do you plan to get there? The wise late Dr. Franklin Covey left us with an incredible body of work. One of his lessons is to *begin with the end in mind.* We will use this concept to successfully career map. By starting with the end in mind, you can successfully pinpoint what is at the core of your heart's desire. By having a clear understanding of what you want out of life, career, finances, relationships, etc., you will be able to set clear intentions to make your dreams match your reality.

APPLICATION 14: Begin with the End in Mind

- To start, think ahead, far ahead, way out to your retirement party. Think of who will be there. Friends, family and loved ones will all be gathered to celebrate all your accomplishments and all that you have become.

- When your loved ones speak about your accomplishments, what will they say about you?

_____
_____
_____
_____
_____

- What did you do for fun?

  _____

  _____

  _____

  _____

- How did you influence other lives?

  _____

  _____

  _____

  _____

- What community outreach work did you do?

  _____

  _____

  _____

  _____

- What charity did you create?

  _____

  _____

  _____

  _____

- What services did you offer to others?

  _____

  _____

  _____

  _____

- What legacy will you be known for?

  _____
  _____
  _____
  _____
  _____

- How did you leave your mark on the world, making it a better place?

  _____
  _____
  _____
  _____
  _____

In her first Oscar acceptance speech, the beautifully gifted actress Lupita Nyong'o stated, "No matter where you are from, your dreams are valid."

This next part of this application is for you to test-drive bigger dreams. This is an opportunity for you to dream big!

- What type of cars did you drive?

  _____
  _____
  _____
  _____
  _____

- How much money did you make?

  _____
  _____

_____

_____

_____

- What did your love life look like?

_____

_____

_____

_____

- Where did you travel?

_____

_____

_____

_____

- What type of clothes did you wear?

_____

_____

_____

_____

- What did you create that will live beyond your years?

_____

_____

_____

_____

- How did you express yourself creatively?

  _____

  _____

  _____

  _____

  _____

- What type of person did you become?

  _____

  _____

  _____

  _____

  _____

- What are three things that you can do right now to become this person right now?

  _____

  _____

  _____

  _____

  _____

If you want to become an author, know that you are already an author. If you want to be an actress, see yourself as an actress right now. If you want to be a business owner, see yourself as that right in this moment. If you want to become a millionaire, act and it is so. Think it. See it. Feel it. Be it. Empower yourself to be who you see yourself as and all things will align themselves to you accordingly. Likeness attracts likeness unto itself. Allow The Law of Attraction to take place and work in your benefit. You don't have to see the entire staircase to take the first step towards making your dreams come true. Simply take one step in the direction that you want to go in.

Now that you have the end in mind clearly written out, you will complete a vision board to visualize exactly what you want out of your life. You can use your vision board as part of your daily ritual to visualize what you want your life to become.

Application Notes

_____

_____

_____

_____

_____

_____

_____

_____

_____

_____

_____

_____

_____

_____

_____

_____

Application Notes

We all have a purpose.
We all have the
capacity to make this
world a better place.

CHAPTER 15

How to Discover Your Purpose

"The purpose of our lives is to be happy." –Dalai Lama

Discovering your purpose takes courage. Discovering your purpose is a reflection of what true strength is. There are many books that you can purchase for advice, but I believe that if you continue to look outside yourself for guidance, you will continue to be pointed in the wrong direction. While books and mentors are necessary and useful, there is a point when you must trust your inner guidance system. Your inner conscience is honest. All you have ever had to do is listen to the voice within and quiet your thoughts so that you can hear. At this stage in your journey, you have developed strong tools to assist you in having a breakthrough. Simply be patient with your growth and gentle with yourself because change takes time. Success happens over nights, not overnight.

In her early 20s, Tina Fey was working the front desk at the YMCA and taking night classes at Second City in Chicago. It wasn't until she turned 27 that she decided to move to New York and her life has never been the same.

Vera Wang failed to make it to the 1968 Olympics and decided to go to fashion school while working at a YSL boutique in New

York. In 1987, she took her talents to Ralph Lauren and worked as a design director. Then, at 41, in 1990, she decided to follow her heart and create her own bridal boutique. Vera never gave up on herself or her dream and she is now creating the life that she loves.

In a survey given to people facing their last days, they were asked what they regretted. The most common answer was that they did not follow the callings of their heart. They encourage people to live their dreams and to stay mindful that each day is a gift to be celebrated. Don't continue to look for a career before you listen for a calling. Do not decide to be happy once you are a success. The key is to be happy now, with what you have and allow that to build momentum. It is very important that you take time to revel in this truth.

Now, let's think about how you can tap into and discover your purpose. Time is certain to pass. This life is a gift from the world. Using and sharing your talents is your gift back to the world. In that spirit, what can you do to ensure that the time you are given is put to good use? How will you leave your mark on this world?

APPLICATION 15: Discover Your Purpose

- What is your soul nudging you to do?

  _____

  _____

  _____

  _____

  _____

- What books do you need to purchase to strengthen your skill set to further your path in the direction you want to go?

  _____

  _____

  _____

  _____

  _____

- What mentors can you connect with who are already where you want to be?

  _____

  _____

  _____

  _____

  _____

- What else can you do to take action and make your dreams come to life?

  _____

  _____

  _____

  _____

  _____

- If you were to form your own company, what products or services would you offer?

  _____

  _____

  _____

  _____

- What would you call your company?

  _____

  _____

  _____

  _____

  _____

- What can you do now to bring your company to life?

  _____

  _____

  _____

  _____

  _____

Pause from reading until you have completed this journal entry

Application Notes

When was the last time
someone created an
opportunity for you to
bring your dream to
life? Guess what? This
is your opportunity.

CHAPTER 16

Develop Self-Mastery

*"Your mind is your instrument. Learn to be
its master and not its slave."* –Rumi

In the article, "4 Steps to Self Mastery", Roger Gabriel explains
what self-mastery is. He writes,

> "Mastery is usually defined as being highly skilled
> or proficient in one or more areas of life. Self-
> Mastery takes this to its highest level. To be the
> Master of your own self is to fully understand
> who you really are. It is a discovery of the Guru
> within, the inner guiding light. It means taking
> full responsibility for your own life. Mastery in
> this sense doesn't mean to control in a negative
> way; it's the realization that you are the Universe,
> and that you and everything around you flows
> harmoniously together in the magnificent dance
> of your own creation."

Success is a natural state offered to everyone who is willing to
take action on his or her goals. In order to continue on the path
of success, identify weak thoughts that do not serve your higher
being and are true distractions from your growth. In order to

prevent negative thinking that holds you back from your destiny, you can utilize a confrontation technique that will overcome negative energy.

In order to successfully use the confrontation technique, have a positive mental attitude and embrace the following:

1. You must be willing to change your thought pattern from negative to positive.
2. You must truly want success and happiness.
3. You must believe that no temporal energy in your mind can stand up to the power that dwells within you.

If you are in alignment with the points above, then you can utilize this technique as often as you need to.

APPLICATION 16: Confrontation Technique – Develop Self Mastery

When weak and low energy enters your mind, you can transmute it by making a direct affirmation saying: The power within me is greater than the power causing me to (insert your negative thought here).

Example 1: If you are feeling overwhelmed and anxious, say: *"The power within me is greater than the power causing me to feel overwhelmed and anxious. I yield my mind and body to the power within me that brings peace to my mind and body. I give thanks to the power of my mind for giving me self-mastery".*

Example 2: If you are feeling anger or frustration, say: *"The power within me is greater than the power causing me to feel angry and frustrated. I yield my mind and body to the power within me that* *brings peace to my mind and body. I give thanks to the power of my mind for giving me self-mastery".*

Vital points to remember in this practice: always begin your confrontation affirmation technique with:

- "The power within me is greater than _____".
- Continue repeating this and attempt to feel the power of your mind taking over.
- After you have felt positive results, give thanks and show gratitude for Self-Mastery.

Here is an alternative chart that will assist in turning negative thoughts into positive ones:

Negative Lower Self Thoughts	Positive Higher Self Thoughts
Self Regression	Self-Mastery
Self-Destruction	Self-Control
Self-Indulgence	Self-Confidence
Self-Doubt	Self-Assurance
Self-Confusion	Self-Growth
Self-Degrading	Self-Awareness
Self-Fear	Self-Progress
Self-Failure	Self-Success
Self-Defeat	Self-Renewal
Self-Denial	Self-choice

Study the chart and embrace it. Know that there are no thoughts other than positive higher self-thoughts. Decide on the powerful positive choices to allow the power that dwells within you to eliminate whatever weaknesses are holding you back from creating the life that you deserve to have – the life of happiness and fulfillment.

Guidance: *"When something difficult or painful happens, always look to see what it makes possible that wouldn't have otherwise been possible. Like a new adventure, a closer friendship, chocolate in your peanut butter. Everything makes you better".* –The Universe

Pause from reading until you have practiced the
confrontation technique several times.

Application Notes

_____

_____

_____

_____

_____

_____

_____

_____

_____

_____

_____

_____

_____

_____

If you want happiness
for an hour, take a nap.
If you want happiness
for a day, go fishing. If
you want happiness for a
year, inherit a fortune. If
you want happiness for a
lifetime, help somebody.
— Chinese Proverb

CHAPTER 17

How to Follow Your Inner Guidance System

*"Who looks outside, dreams. Who looks
inside, awakens."* –Carl Jung

It is important to follow the inner impulses that you will receive from your guidance system. Earlier in the guide, we discussed focusing on <u>why</u> you are doing something, not how you will do it. Each day, simply focus on why you are doing something and do as much as you can with the 24 hours that you are given to propel your dreams, visions, and goals forward. No need to create a long-term action plan. If you can commit to this easy process, your life will begin to change dramatically for the better.

Taking action is simply having faith in yourself. The only thing that is preventing you from taking action is self-doubt. When this happens, use the tools in this guide to deal with the self-doubt. It is your faith that will take you beyond self-doubt to the surety of putting your ideas into action.

There are two selves in every person: the temporary self and the higher self.

1. The "temporary self" has been created by society and usually has a limited appreciation of all the things that are

possible within you. This side of who you are is not your higher self. It is your lower self.

2. **Your "higher self" is who you truly are – your authentic self.** This is the spark of life that causes you to have existence. Dream BIG, Day Dreamer! Put your ideas into action and stay focused on channeling your higher self.

Remember that you are never alone. By keeping attuned to the presence of your higher self, you will always be directed and guided, eager and excited to take action in your life.

APPLICATION 17: Tap into Your Inner Guidance System

- In order to hear from your inner guidance system, write a letter to God/Source/Universe (whatever title you prefer to use).
- Simply write in the middle of the first line, "Dear God."
- Write until you have all that you need to get off your chest on paper.

_____

_____

_____

_____

_____

_____

_____

_____

_____

_____

_____

_____

_____

_____

_____

_____

_____

_____

_____

_____

- Now sit in silence for a few minutes to listen to your inner guidance system. By listening in silence, you will receive the answer you seek.

- After you have paused for a moment, write whatever answer comes to you.

_____

_____

_____

_____

_____

_____

_____

_____

_____

_____

_____

_____

This answer is your inner guidance system directing you.

Guidance: *"Ever wondered why so many people, sometimes virtual strangers, tell you their deepest secrets? It's because when they look into your eyes, they see me. And sharing your secrets with me, as you, reminds them that no matter what they have to say, my love is so much bigger. We're quite the team!" – The Universe*

Pause from reading until you have direction
from your inner guidance system.

Application Notes

_____

_____

_____

_____

_____

_____

_____

_____

_____

_____

_____

_____

_____

_____

_____

I expect good in my
life because God is the
True Life of my being
and reality, this day.

CHAPTER 18

How to Develop a Mindset of Greatness

"Don't downgrade your dreams to match your reality.
Upgrade your beliefs to match your vision." -Unknown

Now that your inner guidance system has directed you, it is time to develop a mindset of greatness.

With prosperity comes influence, and you have important work to do. You will need to prosper so that others will know it is possible and so that you can have the resources to do the work you are here to do while on earth.

The reality is that you <u>must</u> prosper. Your mindset should leave no other option. In order to build this reality for yourself, there is a behavioral system you can adopt and a process you can follow to discipline your attitude towards money.

First, you must believe that money flows to you and through you. Money works for you. You are developing a great relationship with money.

There is a pot of gold waiting for you and you deserve it! Did you know that 74% of millionaires are entrepreneurs? 5% of sales people in America are millionaires. That speaks volumes! These statistics prove that creating your own path is possible. Also, if you have sales ability and an entrepreneurial spirit, you definitely have what it takes to become a millionaire. If you do not have sales experience or an entrepreneurial spirit, these are amazing skills you can develop.

There are seven steps that you can follow to start the path towards financial freedom:

1. Be honest and authentic.
2. Practice self-discipline whenever it is required.
3. Be likable and get along well with people. Be cheerful, nice and optimistic.
4. Have a supportive spouse/partner and channel energy into common goals.
5. Work hard. Start early, work smart, and create value for millions of people.
6. Do only what you love to do! You will never work a day in your life if you do what you love.
7. Sell your ideas. The more persuasive you are at sales, the faster you will become financially independent.

If you are in debt, in addition to prospering, you will make it a priority to get out of debt. According to Dave Ramsey, "The borrower is a slave to the lender".

Here are five steps you can take to get out of debt:

1. Save money. Get your paycheck and pay yourself first, no matter what.
2. Stop borrowing money.
3. Pray and ask your inner guidance system for help.
4. Sell your stuff downsize.
5. Get a part-time job/hustle.

APPLICATION 18: Develop and Practice your Mindset of Greatness

- Develop and practice the skills and habits above religiously.
- Make a firm decision to become financially independent.
- In time and with practice you will become financially free.

Pause from reading until you have practiced
developing a Mindset of Greatness.

Application Notes

_____

_____

_____

_____

_____

_____

_____

_____

_____

_____

_____

_____

_____

_____

_____

Application Notes

_____

_____

_____

_____

_____

_____

_____

_____

_____

_____

_____

_____

_____

_____

_____

_____

Your hard work will
pay off. The right people
will show up. Your
dreams will come true.

CHAPTER 19

The Science of Getting Rich

*"I always knew I was going to be rich. I don't
think I ever doubted it for a minute."*
–Warren Buffet

Now that you have practiced the steps to becoming a millionaire, we will build on your millionaire mindset and continue to plant the seeds in your mind to transform your approach to money and create success.

The Science of Getting Rich is a book written by the New Thought Movement writer Wallace D. Wattles and published in 1910 by the Elizabeth Towne Company. The book is still in print, relevant to this very day, and a concept applied by those who are wealthy. *The Science of Getting Rich* was credited by Rhonda Byrne as one of the inspirations for her popular film and book *The Secret*. As Byrne explained it on the web site of Oprah Winfrey, "Something inside of me had me turn the pages one by one, and I can still remember my tears hitting the pages as I was reading it. It gave me a glimpse of The Secret. It was like a flame inside of my heart. And with every day since, it's just become a raging fire of wanting to share all of this with the world."

According to *USA Today*, Wattles' text is "divided into short, straight-to-the-point chapters that explain how to overcome mental barriers, and how creation, rather than competition, is the hidden key to wealth attraction."

In his work, Wattles explains that by focusing only on what your heart desires and believing unconditionally that those things are yours to have, you connect to the Universe which gave you those desires in the first place and intends for you to fulfill them. His philosophy is at the essence of how we all can attain real fulfillment and inner-peace doing what we love.

You can use *The Science of Getting Rich* to:

- Think creatively, rather than competitively and how this is one of the keys to becoming wealthy
- Set yourself on the right course to obtaining wealth
- Get rich in a ethical way
- Use positive thinking to obtain your desires
- Succeed doing what you want to do

APPLICATION 19: Listen to the audible of *The Science of Getting Rich*

- Listen to the free 2-hour audible version of *The Science of Getting Rich*, by Wallace D. Wattles, on YouTube.
- After listening, do the reflections below:
- What "ah-hah" moments did you have while listening to this audible?

_____

_____

_____

_____

_____

_____

_____

_____

_____

_____

_____

_____

_____

_____

_____

_____

_____

_____

_____

_____

_____

_____

_____

- How has this concept improved your mindset around getting rich?

_____

_____

_____

_____

_____

_____

_____

_____
_____
_____
_____
_____
_____
_____
_____
_____
_____
_____
_____
_____
_____
_____
_____
_____
_____
_____

- In order to be of service and a help to others, you must first help yourself by creating resources of prosperity. What will change in your life when you create and tap into all resources available to you?

_____
_____
_____
_____
_____
_____
_____
_____

_____

_____

_____

_____

_____

_____

_____

_____

_____

_____

_____

_____

Pause from reading further until you have listened to The Science of Getting Rich and completed your reflections.

Application Notes

_____

_____

_____

_____

_____

_____

_____

_____

_____

_____

_____

_____

_____

_____

_____

Application Notes

The people that I admire
didn't try to fit into a
box. They embraced
their uniqueness and
forged their own path.

CHAPTER 20

The Science of Manifestation

"The power of imagination makes us infinite." –John Muir

Manifesting is defined as being clear to the eye or mind. In order to get what you want, you must be clear on what you want and know how to put intentional energy into bringing it to fruition. Yes, you are that powerful! You know that manifesting works for other people, but for some reason, you feel as though you are missing something in order to make it work for you. The truth is that you have what it takes to manifest, you simply need to put the practice into play and learn how to do it.

Jim Carrey was quoted by saying, "I am a total believer. I believe in manifestation. I believe in putting a rocket of desire out in the universe. You get it when you believe you have it. People still sit around and go "When it's gonna come, when it's gonna come" and that's the wrong way. You're facing away from it. You have to go, it's here, it's here, it's here." Jim Carrey used to go on Mulholland drive and visualize seeing himself being a successful actor and getting work from top directors. We attract abundance only when we dissolve our limiting beliefs. Visualize everything you want and feel as if you already have it. This is how you use the law of attraction.

Will Smith was quoted saying, "Our thoughts, our feelings, our dreams, our ideas are physical in the universe. That if we dream something, if we picture something, it adds a physical thrust towards realization that we can put into the universe." Our thoughts and emotions have physical power. When we have a strong desire, the universe conspires in magnificent ways to fulfill our desires. The only thing we need to do is to believe in ourselves.

The truth is that we are powerful creators with the ability to leave a dent in the universe. Don't underestimate this power. The law of attraction proves that we are capable of extraordinary accomplishments given that our intentions are aligned with the source. Imagination is a powerful tool. If you can see yourself reaching your goals, you will achieve them.

The next application will guide you through the manifestation process.

APPLICATION 20: Learn How to Manifest

- Write down in order of importance the things and the conditions that you want.

  _____

  _____

  _____

  _____

  _____

  _____

  _____

  _____

  _____

  _____

_____

_____

_____

_____

_____

_____

_____

_____

_____

_____

_____

_____

_____

- This is the time to set intentions on the actual things you want to happen in your life. Do not put thought into wanting too much; there is no such thing as too much. Be limitless in writing down the exact desires of your heart.

_____

_____

_____

_____

_____

_____

_____

_____

_____

_____

_____

_____

_____

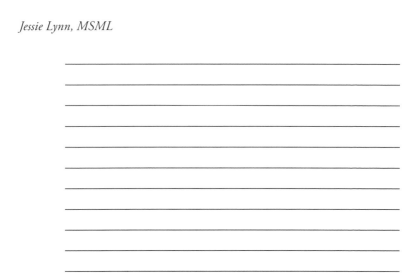

- After you have created your list, look at your list three times a day: morning, noon and night. Think about these things as often as possible.

- Do not share your desires with anyone.

- Use your inner guidance system in your accomplishment of how to get these things done.

- Know that you have the ability to change your list daily. You can add to it and take away from it, and alter it in any way you desire until you have it right.

- Do not be discouraged on account of changes, as change is natural. There will always be changes and additions in your accomplishments and desires.

- As you practice manifestation, you will realize that this is what true faith is all about.

- You will know that your manifestation abilities are at work when new desires, deserving position at or about the top of your list, come to you. When these points occur, pause and express gratitude that you are progressing properly.

When Manifesting:

1. Always stay positive
2. Say it like it's already done
3. Do not spend time thinking about anything opposite of what you want
4. Meditate on what you want
5. See it, smell it, feel it, hear it
6. If it's real in your brain, it will be real in the world

Pause from reading until you have completed
your list of manifestations.

Application Notes

_____

_____

_____

_____

_____

_____

_____

_____

_____

_____

_____

_____

_____

_____

Application Notes

_____

_____

_____

_____

_____

_____

_____

_____

_____

_____

_____

_____

_____

_____

Books + mentors +
goals = success

CHAPTER 21

How to Create a Business Model

*"Take the first step in faith. You don't have to see
the whole staircase, just take the first step."*
–Martin Luther King, Jr.

Now that you have fully completed your list of manifestations, it is time to celebrate this experience! You have come so far and the beauty of this experience is that your journey is not ending, it is actually just beginning. You have so much creating to do! In order to complete this guide, you must now bring your experience full circle and complete your final application.

Now that you have clarity on your business, it is time to take action! Most people take action by creating an action plan. The problem with this system is that the list is crafted and ink is on paper, but the plan never actualizes. You will not do this. You have clarity, you know exactly what it is that you want, and so now you must take action.

You take action by taking one day at a time. Again, do not focus on how you will do anything. When you focus on how you will do something, you will feel angst about it and you do not want that energy around your sacred work. Simply focus on why you are doing it. Why do you want to influence lives? Let that be your driving force. Do as much as you can with the 24 hours that you are given each day.

Focus on why you are doing it.

I created Career Discovery because everyone deserves to operate as his or her best version, have clarity on their life's purpose, and open up revenue streams to support themselves financially. Everyone deserves to have dreams actualized. Everyone deserves to build their own business and leave a legacy in this world.

Why are you creating your company? Take time to reflect on your "why" and let that reason guide you. In this spirit, complete your final application.

APPLICATION 21

Create Your Business Model

Before beginning your Business Model, reflect and write on the questions below:

1. What is your soul calling you to do?

    _____
    _____
    _____
    _____
    _____

2. What do you feel led to do to create change in the world?

    _____
    _____
    _____
    _____
    _____

3. What will you name your company?

_____
_____
_____
_____

4. How do you plan to bring this vision to life?

_____
_____
_____
_____

5. What tools, resources, books, mentors, or training do you need now?

_____
_____
_____
_____
_____

6. What clarity do you have on your passions and purpose?

_____
_____
_____
_____
_____

7. My purpose is to:

_____
_____
_____
_____
_____

You will now create your business model canvas.

Materials needed:

- Poster board
- Different colored post-it notes
- A ruler
- Pen, pencils, markers
- Stickers that inspire you (optional)

How to make your business model canvas:

1. Plot a canvas on a poster board by creating nine large sections/blocks (big enough to hold multiple post-it notes) on the board.
2. Grab your post-it notes.
3. Place your canvas on the wall and sketch out your business model.

There are nine building blocks necessary to structure your business: key partners, key activities, key resources, cost structure, value propositions, customer relationships, channels, customer segments, and revenue streams.

1. **Key Partners:** This block will focus on the network of suppliers and partners that you will need to get your company started. Who are your key partners and what will you need them to do right now? Do you need them to create a business website or a social media campaign? Who will be your key partners to support the growth of your business? These people may be a recruiter, a lead generator, a trainer, a sales team, etc. Write them down on

a sticky note (one sticky note per key partner) and place the notes in the box on your board.

2. **Key Activities:** This block will focus on the most important things your company must do on a daily, weekly, and monthly basis these activities should focus on building your marketing, sales, finance, and operations systems. Realize that your business success will depend 15% on your actual skills and 85% on the systems that you have in place. Think of the marketing, sales, finance, and operation systems as spokes of a tire wheel. These spokes are necessary for your wheel to move forward. Version one is better than Version None. Get your systems in place, allow them to build momentum, and you can assess the effectiveness of each system when the time is right.

3. **Key Resources:** This block will focus on the most important assets that are needed right now. These resources could be the flyers needed to speak to your company, for networking, training tools, etc. You will have the physical, human, intellectual, and financial resources plotted in this section.

4. **Cost Structure:** This block will focus on all the costs that you will incur to make your company work. This covers payroll, marketing, and other costs. This block should highlight your cost driven, value driven, fixed costs, variable costs, economies of scale, and economies of scope. Think about what you will spend money on right now and plot that in your canvas.

5. **Value Propositions:** This block will highlight the bundle of products and services that will create value for your customer segments.

6. **Customer Relationships:** This block will focus on the types of relationships that you will establish with specific customer segments. Will you offer personal assistance? What will your customer experience be like? What will your response plan for each segment be? Will you have automated services?

7. **Channels:** This block will focus on how your company will communicate with its customer segments to deliver the value propositions. Will you use a FedEx or UPS delivery system? Will products ship directly from vendor to client? How will clients receive your services or products?

8. **Customer Segments:** This block will focus on the different groups of people or organizations that you aim to serve. Who are your clients and where are they?

9. **Revenue Streams:** This building block will focus on how your company will generate cash from each customer segment. Will you have products or services (or both) that you will sell? Will you have usage or subscription fees? Will you have training systems? Books? Events?

If you would like support to create your business model, visit www.careerdiscovery.work to book a one-on-one session.

Pause from reading until you have completed
your business model canvas.

Guidance: *"Great big, innovative, world changing ideas are plentiful. People who take tiny little baby steps toward them are rare. You are so acing this life!" –The Universe*

Application Notes

_____

_____

_____

_____

_____

_____

_____

_____

_____

_____

_____

_____

_____

_____

_____

_____

_____

I speak my dreams
into existence

Step into Your Brilliance

With all 21 applications in this guide complete, you have successfully tapped into your inner treasure, which is your divine calling, your purpose.

Beautiful is a woman in alignment with her divine assignment! Congratulations!

As I said at the beginning of this guide, remember that there is always an inner light in you. There is a space where you dwell that is the best version of who you are. There is an inner being that is your best version, your higher self. Master being in this state and do not let anything knock you out of alignment.

Your higher self is the person that the world needs to meet. It is from this space that you will create all that you were born to do. It is from this space that you will allow the spirit of who you truly are to be set free.

Step into your brilliance.

Your passions and purposes are aligned and you are set to leave your mark on the world!

If you would like more support, visit www.careerdiscovery.work and book a one-on-one session.

Further Guidance

- Listen to Binaural Beats at night before bed to promote to healthy brain function.
- Replace music in the car with inspirational audio books of your interest.
- Focus on positive messaging.
- Eliminate all forms of toxicity in your life. Allow your inner guidance system to direct you.
- Do your morning ritual routine daily.
- Meditate for at least 10 minutes each day. I recommend using the Headspace or Calm apps or any other app that you like that is easy for you to access and use daily.
- Commit to evolving into a stronger version of who you are. Embrace the concept of Self Mastery.
- Read books that you love. I recommend: *Rise Sister Rise* and *Light is the New Black,* both by Rebecca Campbell. For entrepreneurs, I recommend *Wiser and Wilder* by Kaya Singer and *Tools for Titans* by Tim Ferris.
- Remain open to mentorship and get a business coach ASAP! Every successful person that you can think of has a support system of mentors and coaches, myself included.
- Give this book to those who are in need of a breakthrough. Whom do you know that will benefit from reading this book?
- For inspiration, follow my Instagram accounts: @ drjessielynn and @careerdiscovery

I can reinvent myself
as many times as I
want. With growth,
there are always new
levels to reach, always.

From the Author

My heart is so full. I am grateful that you took the time to journey along and I am excited to see you make an impact on the world in your own special way. My spirit goes by the name, Jessie Lynn, and I am the founder and mentor at Career Discovery. If you have a few more minutes to spare, I'd like to share a little more with you.

I want to come clean and admit that I spent many years of my life in the wrong career. Not knowing what calling I had on my life, I worked several retail management jobs and even successfully climbed the corporate ladder. If you looked at my paycheck, and my resume, you would think that I was a success like most top-ranked business professionals.

After I completed my master's degree, I started to feel incomplete and unfulfilled with my line of work. I ended my master's journey with a degree in hand but also with a clouded mind about what my life's purpose was. I noticed that many of my fellow peers at college graduated with the same feeling – high levels of uncertainty and a lack of clarity about what their career path should be. For this reason, I made the decision to do very deep interpersonal work, the same work outlined in this guide, and it took me on a journey that changed the course of my life.

The decision to do ***The Work***, single handedly, was one of the best decisions that I ever made. Leading up to my breakthrough, I completed deep interpersonal reflections that led me to realize that I had a passion for mentorship. I also had a passion for business development. I would often embrace others, offer career advice, and leverage my business acumen skills to colleagues as they started small business ventures of their own.

It was the natural passion desire to help others succeed in their career that resulted in the birth of my company, Career Discovery.

Following my dreams, becoming a mother, a mentor, a business woman, an author, and experiencing my dreams actualize, one by one, has been an amazing journey. This journey took place all because I refused to believe that I was put on this earth to simply climb the corporate ladder or chase a company's sales goal. I embarked on a two-year journey completing all of the applications that are listed in this guide and I had a major breakthrough. My hope is that you too have a breakthrough and reach out and share how this guide has affected your life.

Remember to control the energy around you, set your intentions, do your daily rituals and believe that everything is always working out for you.

You are strong. You are brilliant. You are perfection personified. You are going to have contrast to happiness and that is okay. Contrast does not mean that you are off your path. It means that you are on your path, and it allows you to stay mindful of what you want and do not want out of life.

Like The Alchemist, there will be signs and wonders all around you. You will notice synchronicities. You will even notice that numbers will start to repeat in patterns. The mysteries of the Universe are truly magical. Pay attention to everything, because your journey is a continuous unfoldment.

You are right where you need to be and the timing is perfect for you to be your true authentic self. Authenticity is the new beautiful. Embrace who you are, stay disciplined and focus, and continue to do the work leaving your own mark on this world! As you do your work, know that I am journeying on with you doing my work as well.

Ashe.

Personal Acknowledgements - With Gratitude

To my catalyst for growth, The Universe.
Thank you for the lessons, for your unconditional love, and for being a mirror reflecting all that I AM.

To my beloved daughter, Ava Lynn Montgomery:
Thank you for being mommy's "Why". Thank you for changing the trajectory of my life. Thank you for all of your 3s. Thank you for the magic that you are. You call me to my greatness in your own special way and I am grateful that you chose me to be your mommy. You are my Universe.

To my family, friends, and teachers that I met along my path:
Thank you for pouring your time, knowledge, love, and wisdom into me. I am grateful that you are a part of my life.

To The Universe:
I am that I am.

Application Notes

May this LIGHT
continue to SHINE.
I let it be.
And so it is.

Printed in the United States
By Bookmasters